POPULAR CULTURE IN AMERICA

1800-1925

POPULAR CULTURE IN AMERICA

1800-1925

Advisory Editor
DAVID MANNING WHITE

Editorial Board
RAY B. BROWNE
MARSHALL W. FISHWICK
RUSSEL B. NYE

CAPTIVITY TALES

ARNO PRESS

A New York Times Company

New York · 1974

Reprint Edition 1974 by Arno Press Inc.

Reprinted from copies in the State
Historical Society of Wisconsin and
University of Illinois Libraries

POPULAR CULTURE IN AMERICA: 1800-1925
ISBN for complete set: 0-405-06360-1
See last pages of this volume for titles.

Publisher's Notes: The contributions in
this anthology were reprinted from the
best available copies. The pagination of
Miss Annie Coleson's Narrative is irregular.
All copies seen were identical. The book is
complete as reprinted here.

Manufactured in the United States of America

———◆———

Library of Congress Cataloging in Publication Data
Main entry under title:

Captivity tales.

(Popular culture in America)
Reprint of Indian atrocities: narratives of the
perils and sufferings of Dr. Knight and John Slover
among the Indians during the Revolutionary War, with
short memoirs of Col. Crawford and John Slover, and a
letter from H. Brackinridge on the rights of the Indians,
etc., by H. H. Brackinridge, first published in 1867
in Cincinnati: an interesting and remarkable account
of the terrible sufferings and providential escape of
Miss Ann Coleson, a victim of the late Indian outrages
in Minnesota, by A. Coleson, first published in 1864 by
Barclay, Philadelphia; of The dangers and sufferings of
Robert Eastburn, and his deliverance from Indian captivity, with introd. and notes by John R. Spears, by
R. Eastburn, first published in 1904 by Burrows Bros.
Co., Cleveland; and of A narrative of the wonderful
escape and dreadful sufferings of Colonel James Paul,
after the defeat of Col. Crawford, when that unfortu-
nate commander, and many of his men, were inhumanly
burnt at the stake, and others were slaughtered by
other modes of torture known only to savages, by
J. Paul, first printed in 1869 by Spiller, Cincinnati.
   1. Indians of North America--Captivities.
I. Series.
E85.C26 1974   970.3   74-15729
ISBN 0-405-06365-2

CONTENTS

Indian Atrocities.

NARRATIVES

OF THE

PERILS AND SUFFERINGS

OF

DR. KNIGHT AND JOHN SLOVER,

AMONG THE INDIANS,

DURING THE

REVOLUTIONARY WAR,

WITH SHORT MEMOIRS OF

COL. CRAWFORD & JOHN SLOVER.

AND A LETTER FROM H. BRACKINRIDGE, ON THE RIGHTS OF
THE INDIANS, ETC.

CINCINNATI:

U. P. JAMES, PUBLISHER.

[*Reprinted from the Nashville edition of 1843.*]

1867.

PUBLISHER'S NOTICE.

The first edition of these Narratives was printed in Pittsburgh, in 1782, in pamphlet form : a copy can hardly be procured now at any price. Another small edition was printed in Nashville in 1843, which has become exceedingly scarce. It is hoped this reprint may prove acceptable to all interested in the early history of our country, and struggles of the Pioneers with the Indians.

Five hundred copies only, (letter press) are printed of this edition.

U. P. JAMES,

Cincinnati, O., 1867.

TO THE PUBLIC.

THE two following Narratives were transmitted for publication in September last, but shortly afterwards the letters from Sir Guy Carlton, to his Excellency, General Washington, informing that the Savages had received orders to desist from their incursions, gave reason to hope that there would be an end to their barbarities. For this reason it was not thought necessary to hold up to view what they had heretofore. done. But as they still continue their murders on our frontier, these Narratives may be serviceable to induce our government to take some effectual steps to chastise and suppress them; as from hence they will see that the nature of an

Indian is fierce and cruel, and that an extirpation of them would be useful to the world, and honorable to those who can effect it.

August 3, 1782.

LETTER.

MR. BAILY:

Enclosed are two Narratives, one of Dr. Knight, who acted as Surgeon in the expedition under Col. Crawford, the other of John Slover. That of Dr. Knight was written by himself at my request; that of Slover was taken by myself from his mouth as he related it.

This man, from his childhood, lived amongst the Indians; though perfectly sensible and intelligent, yet he cannot write. The character of Dr. Knight is well known to be that of a good man, of strict veracity, of a calm and deliberate mind, and using no exaggeration in his account of any matter.

As a testimony in favor of the veracity of Slover, I thought proper to procure a certificate from the Clergyman to whose church he belongs, and which I give below.

H. BRACKINRIDGE.

———

" I do hereby certify that John Slover has been for many years a regular member of the church under my care, and is worthy of the highest credit.

WILLIAM RENO."

Pittsburg, August 3, 1782.

THE

NARRATIVE OF DR. KNIGHT.

BOUT the latter end of the month of March or the beginning of April, of the present year, (1781) the western Indians began to make incursions upon the frontiers of Ohigan and Washington, Youghugany and Westmorlean counties, which has been their constant practice ever since the commencement of the present war between the United States and Great Britain.

In consequence of these predatory invasions, the principal officers of the above mentioned counties, namely : Colonels Williamson and Marshall, tried every method in their power to

2

set on foot an expedition against the Wyandot towns, which they could effect no other way than by giving all possible encouragement to volunteers. The plan proposed was as follows: Every man furnishing himself with a horse, a gun, and one month's provisions, should be exempt from two tours of militia duty. Likewise, that every one who had been plundered by the Indians, should, if the plunder could be found at their towns, have it again, proving it to be his property, and all horses lost on the expedition by unavoidable accident were to be replaced by horses taken in the enemy's country.

The time appointed for the rendezvous, or general meeting of the volunteers, was fixed to be on the 20th of May, and the place, the old Mingo town, on the west side of the river Ohio, about forty miles below Fort Pitt, by land; and I think about seventy-five by water.

Col. Crawford was solicited by the general voice of these western counties and districts to command the expedition. He accordingly set out as a volunteer, and came to Fort Pitt two days before the time appointed for the assembling of the men. As there was no

Surgeon yet appointed to go with the expedition, Col. Crawford begged the favor of Gen. Irvin to permit me to accompany him, (my consent having been previously asked,) to which the General agreed, provided Col. Gibson did not object.

Having obtained permission of the Col., I left Fort Pitt on Tuesday, May 1st, and the next day about one in the afternoon, arrived at the Mingo bottom.

The volunteers had not all crossed the river until Friday morning, the 24th, they then distributed themselves into eighteen companies, choosing their captains by vote. There were chosen also, one Col. Commandant, four field and one brigadier Major. There were four hundred and sixty-five that voted.

We began our march on Saturday, May 25th, making almost a due West course, and on the fourth day reach the old Moravian town, upon the river Muskingum, about 60 miles from the river Ohio. Some of the men having lost their horses on the night preceding, returned home.

Thursday the 28th in the evening, Major Brenton and Captain Bean, went some distance from camp to reconnoitre; having gone about one quarter of a mile they saw two Indians, upon whom they fired, and then retreated to camp. This was the first place in which we were discovered, as we understood afterwards.

On Thursday the 4th of June, which was the eleventh day of our march, about one o'clock we came to the spot where the town of Sandusky formerly stood; the inhabitants had moved 18 miles lower down the creek nearer the lower Sandusky; but as neither our guides or any who were with us had known any thing of their removal, we began to conjecture, there were no Indian towns nearer than the lower Sandusky, which was at least forty miles distant.

However, after refreshing our horses we advanced on search of some of their settlements, but had scarcely got the distance of three or four miles from the old town when a number of our men expressed their desire to return, some of them alleging that they had only five days provisions; upon which the field Officers and Captains, determined in council, to proceed that afternoon and no longer. Previous to the calling of this council, a small party of light horse had been sent forward to reconnoitre.

I shall here remark by the way, that there

are a great many extensive plains in that country. The woods in general grow very thin, and free from brush and underwood; so that light horsemen may advance a considerable distance before an army without being much exposed to the enemy.

Just as the council decided, an express returned from the above mentioned party of light horse with intelligence that they had been about three miles in front, and had seen a large body of Indians running towards them. In a short time we saw the rest of the light horse, who joined us, and having gone one mile further, met a number of Indians who had partly got possession of a piece of woods before us, whilst we were in the plains; but our men alighting from their horses and rushing into the woods, soon obliged them to abandon that place.

The enemy being by this time reinforced, flanked to the right, and part of them coming in nearer, quickly made the action more serious. The firing continued very warm on both sides from four o'clock until the dusk of the evening, each party maintaining their ground. Next morning, about six o'clock, their guns were discharged, at the distance of two or three hundred yards, which continued till day, doing little or no execution on either side.

The field officers then assembled and agreed, as the enemy were every moment increasing, and we had already a number of wounded, to retreat that night. The whole body was to form into three lines, keeping the wounded in the centre. We had four killed and twenty-three wounded, of the latter, seven very dangerously, on which account as many biers were got ready to carry them; most of the rest were slightly wounded and none so bad but they could ride on horseback. After dark the officers went on the out-posts and brought in all the men as expeditiously as they could. Just as the troops were about to form, several guns were fired by the enemy, upon which some of our men spoke out and said, our intention was discovered by the Indians who were firing alarm guns. Upon which some in front hurried off and the rest immediately followed, leaving the seven men that were dangerously wounded, some of whom however got off on horseback, by means of some good friends, who waited for, and assisted them.

We had not got a quarter of a mile from

the field of action when I heard Col. Crawford calling for his son, John Crawford, his son-in-law, Major Harrison, Major Rose and Wm. Crawford, his nephews, upon which I came up and told him I believed they were on before us. He asked was that the doctor? I told him it was. He then replied they were not in front, and begged of me not to leave him. I promised him I would not.

We then waited and continued calling for these men till the troops had passed us. The Colonel told me his horse had almost given out, that he could not keep up with the troops, and wished some of his best friends to remain with him. He then exclaimed against the militia for riding off in such an irregular manner, and leaving some of the wounded behind, contrary to his orders. Presently there came two men riding after us, one of them an old man, the other a lad. We enquired if they had seen any of the above persons? They answered they had not.

By this time there was a very hot firing before us, and as we judged, near where our main body must have been. Our course was then nearly Southwest, but changing it, we went north about two miles, the two men remaining

in company with us. Judging ourselves to be
now out of the enemy's lines, we took a due
East course, taking care to keep at the distance
of fifteen or twenty yards apart, and directing
ourselves by the North star.

The old man often lagged behind, and when
this was the case, never failed to call for us to
halt for him. When we were near the Sandusky
creek he fell one hundred yards behind, and
bawled out, as usual, for us to halt. While we
were preparing to reprimand him for making
a noise, I heard an Indian halloo, as I thought,
one hundred and fifty yards from the man,
and partly behind him. After this we did not
hear the man call again, neither did he ever
come up to us any more. It was now past
midnight, and about daybreak Col. Crawford's
and the young man's horses gave out, and they
left them. We pursued our journey East-
ward, and about two o'clock fell in with Capt.
Biggs, who had carried Lieut. Ashley from the
field of action, who had been dangerously
wounded. We then went on about the space
of an hour, when a heavy rain coming on, we
concluded it was best to encamp, as we were
encumbered with the wounded officer. We then
barked four or five trees, made an encampment

and a fire, and remained there all that night. Next morning we again prosecuted our journey, and having gone about three miles found a deer which had been recently killed. The meat was sliced from the bones and bundled up in the skin, with a tomahawk lying by it. We carried all with us, and in advancing about one mile further, espied the smoke of a fire. We then gave the wounded officer into the charge of the young man, directing him to stay behind whilst the Colonel, the Captain and myself walked up as cautiously as we could toward the fire. When we came to it, we concluded, from several circumstances, some of our people had encamped there the preceding night. We then went about roasting the venison, and when just about to march, observed one of our men coming upon our tracks. He seemed at first very shy, but having called to him, he came up and told us he was the person who had killed the deer, but upon hearing us come up, was afraid of Indians, hid it in a thicket and made off. Upon this we gave him some bread and roasted venison, proceeded all together on our journey, and about two o'clock came upon the paths by which we had gone out. Capt. Biggs and myself did not think it safe to keep the road, but the Colonel said the Indians would not follow the troops farther than the plains, which we were then considerably past. As the wounded officer rode Capt. Biggs' horse, I lent the Captain mine. The Colonel and myself went about one hundred yards in front, the Captain and the wounded officer in the centre, and the two young men behind. After we had traveled about one mile and a half, several Indians started up within fifteen or twenty steps of the Colonel and me. As we at first discovered only three, I immediately got behind a large black oak, made ready my piece and raised it up to take sight, when the Colonel called to me twice not to fire, upon that one of the Indians ran up to the Colonel and took him by the hand.

They were Delaware Indians of the Wingenim tribe. Captain Biggs fired amongst them but did no execution. They then told us to call these people and make them come there, else they would go and kill them, which the Colonel did, but they forgot us and escaped for that time. The Colonel and I were then taken to the Indian camp, which was about half a mile from the place where we were captured. On Sunday evening five Delawares who had posted themselves at some distance further on the road brought back to the camp, where we lay, Captain Biggs' and Lieutenant Ashley's scalps, with an Indian scalp which Captain Biggs had taken in the field of action; they also brought in Biggs' horse and mine, they told us the other two men got away from them.

Monday morning the tenth of June, we were paraded to march to Sandusky, about thirty-three miles distant; they had eleven prisoners of us and four scalps, the Indians being seventeen in number.

Col. Crawford was very desirous to see a certain Simon Girty, who lived with the Indians, and was on this account permitted to go to town the same night, with two warriors to guard him, having orders at the same time to pass by the place where the Col. had turned out his horse, that they might if possible, find him. The rest of us were taken as far as the old town which was within eight miles of the new.

Tuesday morning, the eleventh, Col. Crawford was brought out to us on purpose to be marched in with the other prisoners. I asked the Col. if he had seen Mr. Girty? He told me he had, and that Girty had promised to do every thing in his power for him, but that the Indians were very much enraged against the prisoners; particularly Captain Pipe one of the chiefs; he likewise told me that Girty had informed him that his son-in-law Col. Harrison and his nephew William Crawford, were made prisoners by the Shawanese, but had been pardoned. This Captain Pipe had come from the town about an hour before Col. Crawford, and had painted all the prisoner's faces black. As he was painting me he told me I should go to the Shawanese towns and see my friends. When the Col. arrived he painted him black also, told him he was glad to see him and that he would have him shaved when he came to see his friends at the Wyandot town. When we marched the Col. and I were kept back between Pipe and Wyngenim, the two Delaware chiefs, the other nine prisoners were sent forward with another party of Indians. As we went along we saw four of the prisoners lying by the path tomahawked and scalped, some of them were at the distance of half a mile from each other. When we arrived within half a mile of the place where the Col. was executed, we overtook the five prisoners that remained alive; the Indians had caused them to sit down on the ground, as they did also the Col. and me at some distance from them. I was there given in charge to an Indian fellow to be taken to the Shawanese towns.

In the place where we were now made to sit down there was a number of squaws and boys, who fell on the five prisoners and tomahawked them. There was a certain John McKinly amongst the prisoners, formerly an officer in the 13th Virginia regiment, whose head an old squaw cut off, and the Indians kicked it about upon the ground. The young Indian fellows came often where the Col. and I were, and dashed the scalps in our faces. We were then conducted along toward the place where the Col. was afterwards executed ; when we came within about half a mile of it, Simon Girty met us, with several Indians on horseback ; he spoke to the Col., but as I was about one hundred and fifty yards behind could not hear what passed between them.

Almost every Indian we met struck us either with sticks or their fists. Girty waited till I was brought up and asked, was that the doctor ?—I told him yes, and went toward him

reaching out my hand, but he bid me begone
and called me a damned rascal, upon which
the fellows who had me in charge pulled me
along.   Girty rode up after me and told me I
was to go to the Shawanese towns.

When we went to the fire the Col. was stripped naked, ordered to sit down by the fire and
then they beat him with sticks and their fists.
Presently after I was treated in the same manner.   They then tied a rope to the foot of a
post about fifteen feet high, bound the Col's
hands behind his back and fastened the rope
to the ligature between his wrists.   The rope
was long enough for him to sit down or walk
round the post once or twice and return the
same way.   The Col. then called to Girty and
asked if they intended to burn him ?—Girty
answered, yes.   The Col. said he would take
it all patiently.   Upon this Captain Pipe, a
Delaware chief, made a speech to the Indians,
viz.: about thirty or forty men, sixty or seventy
squaws and boys.

When the speech was finished they all yelled
a hideous and hearty assent to what had been
said.   The Indian men then took up their guns
and shot powder into the Colonel's body, from
his feet as far up as his neck.   I think not

less than seventy loads were discharged upon his naked body. They then crowded about him, and to the best of my observation, cut off his ears; when the throng had dispersed a little I saw the blood running from both sides of his head in consequence thereof.

The fire was about six or seven yards from the post to which the Colonel was tied; it was made of small hickory poles, burnt quite through in the middle, each end of the poles remaining about six feet in length. Three or four Indians by turns would take up, individually, one of these burning pieces of wood and apply it to his naked body, already burnt black with the powder. These tormentors presented themselves on every side of him with the burning faggots and poles. Some of the squaws took broad boards, upon which they would carry a quantity of burning coals and hot embers and throw on him, so that in a short time he had nothing but coals of fire and hot ashes to walk upon.

In the midst of these extreme tortures, he called to Simon Girty and begged of him to shoot him; but Girty making no answer he called to him again. Girty then, by way of derision, told the Colonel he had no gun, at the same time turning about to an Indian who was behind him, laughed heartily, and by all his gestures seemed delighted at the horrid scene.

Girty then came up to me and bade me prepare for death. He said, however, I was not to die at that place, but to be burnt at the Shawanese towns. He swore by G——d I need not expect to escape death, but should suffer it in all its extremities.

He then observed, that some prisoners had given him to understand, that if our people had had him they would not hurt him; for his part, he said, he did not believe it, but desired to know my opinion of the matter, but being at that time in great anguish and distress for the torments the Colonel was suffering before my eyes, as well as the expectation of undergoing the same fate in two days, I made little or no answer. He expressed a great deal of ill will for Col. Gibson, and said he was one of his greatest enemies, and more to the same purpose, to all which I paid very little attention.

Col. Crawford at this period of his sufferings besought the Almighty to have mercy on his soul, spoke very low, and bore his torments with the most manly fortitude. He continued in all the extremities of pain for an hour and three-quarters or two hours longer, as near as I can judge, when at last, being almost exhausted, he lay down on his belly; they then scalped him and repeatedly threw the scalp in my face, telling me "that was my great captain." An old squaw (whose appearance every way answered the ideas people entertain of the Devil,) got a board, took a parcel of coals and ashes and laid them on his back and head, after he had been scalped, he then raised himself upon his feet and began to walk round the post; they next put a burning stick to him as usual, but he seemed more insensible of pain than before.

The Indian fellow who had me in charge, now took me away to Capt. Pipe's house, about three-quarters of a mile from the place of the Colonel's execution. I was bound all night, and thus prevented from seeing the last of the horrid spectacle. Next morning, being June 12th, the Indian untied me, painted me black, and we set off for the Shawanese town, which he told me was somewhat less than forty miles from that place. We soon came to the spot where the Colonel had been burnt, as it was

3

partly in our way; I saw his bones lying amongst the remains of the fire, almost burnt to ashes; I suppose after he was dead they had laid his body on the fire.

The Indian told me that was my Big Captain, and gave the scalp halloo. He was on horseback and drove me before him.

I pretended to this Indian I was ignorant of the death I was to die at the Shawanese towns, assumed as cheerful a countenance as possible, and asked him if we were not to live together as brothers in one house when we should get to the town? He seemed well pleased, and said yes. He then asked me if I could make a wigwam?—·I told him I could—he then seemed more friendly. We went that day as near as I can judge about 25 miles, the course partly Southwest.—The Indian told me we should next day come to the town, the sun being in such a direction, pointing nearly South. At night, when we went to rest, I attempted very often to untie myself, but the Indian was extremely vigilant and scarcely ever shut his eyes that night. About daybreak he got up and untied me; he next began to mend up the fire, and as the gnats were troublesome I asked him if I should make a smoke behind him—he said yes. I then took the end of a dogwood fork which had been burnt down to about 18 inches long; it was the longest stick I could find, yet too small for the purpose I had in view; then I picked up another smaller stick and taking a coal of fire between them went behind him; then turning suddenly about, I struck him on the head with all the force I was master of; which so stunned him that he fell forward with both his hands into the fire, but seeing him recover and get up, I seized his gun while he ran off howling in a most fearful manner. I followed him with a determination to shoot him down, but pulling back the cock of the gun with too great violence, I believe I broke the main spring. I pursued him, however, about thirty yards, still endeavoring to fire the gun, but could not; then going back to the fire I took his blanket, a pair of new moccasins, his hoppes, powder horn, bullet bag, (together with the gun) and marched off, directing my course toward the five o'clock mark; about half an hour before sunset I came to the plains which I think are about sixteen miles wide. I laid me down in a thicket till dark, and then by the assistance of the north star made my way through them and got into the woods before morning. I proceeded on the next day, and about noon crossed the paths by which our troops had gone out; these paths are nearly East and West, but I went due North all that afternoon with a view to avoid the enemy.

In the evening I began to be very faint, and no wonder; I had been six days prisoner; the last two days of which I had eat nothing, and but very little the first three or four; there were wild gooseberries in abundance in the woods, but being unripe, required mastication, which at that time I was not able to perform on account of a blow received from an Indian on the jaw with the back of a tomahawk. There was a weed that grew plentifully in that place, the juice of which I knew to be grateful and nourishing; I gathered a bundle of the same, took up my lodging under a large spreading beech tree and having sucked plentifully of the juice, went to sleep. Next day, I made a due East course which I generally kept the rest of my journey. I often imagined my gun was only wood bound, and tried every method I could devise to unscrew the lock but never could effect it, having no knife nor any thing fitting for the purpose. I had now the satisfaction to find my jaw began to mend, and in four or five days could chew any vegetable proper for nourishment, but finding my gun only a useless burden, left it in the wilderness. I had no apparatus for making fire to sleep by, so that I could get but little rest for the gnats and musketoes; there are likewise a great many swamps in the beech ridge, which occasioned me very often to lie wet; this ridge, through which I traveled, is about 20 miles broad, the ground in general very level and rich, free from shrubs and brush; there are, however, very few springs, yet wells might easily be dug in all parts of the ridge; the timber on it is very lofty, but it is no easy matter to make a straight course through the same, the moss growing as high upon the South side of the trees as on the North. There are a great many white oaks, ash and hickory trees that grow among the beech timber; there are likewise some places on the ridge, perhaps for three or four continued miles where there is little or no beech, and in such spots, black, white oak, ash and hickory abound. Sugar trees grow there also to a very great bulk— the soil is remarkably good, the ground a little ascending and descending with some small

rivulets and a few springs. When I got out
of the beech ridge and nearer the river Muskingum, the lands were more broken but equally
rich with those before mentioned, and abound-
ing with brooks and springs of water; there
are also several small creeks that empty into
that river, the bed of which is more than a
mile wide in many places; the woods consist
of white and black oak, walnut, hickory and
sugar tree in the greatest abundance. In
all parts of the country through which I
came the game was very plenty, that is to
say, deer, turkies and pheasants; I likewise
saw a great many vestiges of bears and some
elks.

I crossed the river Muskingum about
three or four miles below Fort Lawrence, and
crossing all paths aimed for the Ohio river.
All this time my food was gooseberries, young
nettles, the juice of herbs, a few service
berries, and some May apples, likewise two
young blackbirds and a terrapin, which I
devoured raw. When my food sat heavy on
my stomach, I used to eat a little wild ginger
which put all to rights.

I came upon the Ohio river about five miles
below Fort McIntosh, in the evening of the

21st day after I had made my escape, and on the 22d about seven o'clock in the morning, being the fourth day of July, arrived safe, though very much fatigued, at the Fort.

A SHORT MEMOIR

OF

COL. CRAWFORD.

 OLONEL Crawford, was about
50 years of age, had been an
old warrior against the savages. He distinguished himself early as a volunteer in
the last war, and was taken
notice of by Colonel [now general] Washington, who procured for him the commission of
ensign. As a partisan he showed himself
very active, and was greatly successful. He
took several Indian towns, and did great service in scouting, patrolling and defending the
frontiers. At the commencement of this war
he raised a regiment in the back country by

his own exertions.   He had the commission of
Colonel in the continental army, and acted bravely on several occasions in the years 1776, 1777,
and at other times.   He held his commission
at the time he took command of the militia,
in the aforesaid expedition against the Indians; most probably he had it with him
when he was taken.   He was a man of good
judgment, singular good nature, and great
humanity, and remarkable for his hospitality,
few strangers coming to the western country,
and not spending some days at the crossing of
the Yohagany river, where he lived; no man
therefore could be more regretted.

MEMOIR

OF

JOHN SLOVER.

 HE circumstances that took place, previous to his being taken a prisoner by the Indians the first time, when he was only eight years old, as related by his older brother, Abraham. My father's residence was on New river, Virginia; the Indians came to my father's house, he being absent; we were a short distance from the house; on discovering the Indians there, the smaller children all ran to the bouse; while I turned my course through a meadow to a thick place of woods: when I came near the woods I turned my eyes and saw two Indians

pursuing me. I escaped, and they returned to the house. They took my mother, brother, and sisters prisoners, plundered the house, and took all they could carry; then they took up the line of march. But they had not gone far before my father came home, and seeing the devastation about the house, his family all gone, being well assured it was the work of the savages, it was too much for human nature to bear. He hallooed; the Indians hearing him, they all stopped; two warriors went back with their guns, and in a short time my mother heard the report of a gun; in a few minutes they returned with the horse and saddle my father was riding; my mother knew her husband was killed.

They then went on their journey towards the Indian towns, having nothing to eat but wild meats; through the fatigue of the journey, the two youngest children died in the wilderness.

Our mother was exchanged after a number of years, and returned, and lived with her children; she shortly afterwards died.

John Slover died near Red Banks, Kentucky, at an advanced age, leaving seven children, some of whom are now living.

THE NARRATIVE

OF

JOHN SLOVER.

AVING in the last war been a prisoner amongst the Indians many years, and so being well acquainted with the country west of the Ohio, I was employed as a guide in the expedition under Col. William Crawford against the Indian towns on or near the river Sandusky. It will be unnecessary for me to relate what is so well known, the circumstances and unfortunate events of that expedition; it will be sufficient to observe, that having on Tuesday the fourth of June, fought the enemy near Sandusky, we lay that night in our camp, and the next day fired on each

other at the distance of three hundred yards, doing little or no execution. In the evening of that day it was proposed by Col. Crawford, as I have been since informed, to draw off with order; but at the moment of our retreat the Indians (who had probably perceived that we were about to retreat) firing alarm guns, our men broke and rode off in confusion, treading down those who were on foot, and leaving the wounded men who supplicated to be taken with them.

I was with some others on the rear of our troops feeding our horses in the glade, when our men began to break. The main body of our people had passed by me a considerable distance before I was ready to set out. I overtook them before they crossed the glade, and was advanced almost in front. The company in which I was had separated from me, and had endeavored to pass a morass, for coming up I found their horses had stuck fast in the morass, and endeavoring to pass, mine also in a short time stuck fast. I ought to have said, the company of five or six men with which I had been immediately connected, and who were some distance to the right of the main body, had separated from me, &c. I tried a long

time to disengage my horse, until I could hear
the enemy just behind me, and on each side,
but in vain.   Here then I was obliged to leave
him. The morass was so unstable that I was to
the middle in it, and it was with the greatest
difficulty that I got across it, but which having
at length done, I came up with the six men
who had left their horses in the same manner
I had done; two of these, my companions,
having lost their guns.

We traveled that night, making our course
towards Detroit, with a view to shun the
enemy, who we conceived to have taken the
paths by which the main body of our people
had retreated.   Just before day we got into a
second deep morass, and were under the necessity of delaying until it was light to see our
way through it.   The whole of this day we
traveled towards the Shawanese towns, with a
view of throwing ourselves still farther out of
the search of the enemy.   About ten o'clock
this day we sat down to eat a little, having
tasted nothing from Tuesday, the day of our
engagement, until this time which was on
Thursday, and now the only thing we had to
eat was a scrap of pork to each.   We had sat
down by a warrior's path which we had not

suspected, when eight or nine warriors appeared. Running off hastily we left our baggage and provisions, but were not discovered by the party; for skulking some time in the grass and bushes, we returned to the place and recovered our baggage. The warriors had hallooed as they passed, and were answered by others on our flanks.

In our journey through the glades, or wide extended dry meadows, about twelve o'clock this day, we discovered a party of Indians in front, but skulking in the grass and bushes were not perceived by them. In these glades we were in great danger, as we could be seen at a great distance. In the afternoon of this day there fell a heavy rain, and then traveling on we saw a party of the enemy about two hundred yards before us, but hiding ourselves in the bushes we had again the good fortune not to be discovered. This night we got out of the glades, having in the night crossed the paths by which we had advanced to Sandusky.

It was our design to leave all these paths to the right and to come in by the Tuscarawas. We would have made a much greater progress, had it not been for two of our companions who were lame, the one having his foot burnt, the other with a swelling in his knee of a rheumatic nature.

On this day, which was the second after the retreat, one of our company, the person affected with the rheumatic swelling, was left behind some distance in a swamp. Waiting for him some time we saw him coming within one hundred yards, as I sat on the body of an old tree mending my moccasins, but taking my eye from him. I saw him no more. He had not observed our tracks, but had gone a different way. We whistled on our chargers, and afterwards hallooed for him, but in vain. Nevertheless he was fortunate in missing us, for he afterwards came safe into Wheeling, which is a post of ours on the Ohio, about 70 miles below Fort Pitt. We traveled on until night, and were on the waters of the Muskingum from the middle of this day.

Having caught a fawn this day, we made fire in the evening and had a repast, having in the meantime eat nothing but the small bit of pork I mentioned before. We set off at break of day. About nine o'clock the third day we fell in with a party of the enemy about 12 miles from the Tuscarawas, which is about 135 miles from Fort Pitt. They had come upon our tracks or had been on our flanks and discovered us, and then having got before, had wavlaid us, and fired before we perceived them. At the first fire one of my companions fell before me and another just behind me; these two had guns; there were six men in company, and four guns, two of these rendered useless by reason of the wet when coming through the swamp the first night; we had tried to discharge them but could not. When the Indians fired I ran to a tree, but an Indian presenting himself fifteen yards before me, directed me to deliver myself up and I should not be hurt. My gun was in good order, but apprehending the enemy behind might discharge their pieces at me, I did not risk firing, which I had afterwards reason to regret when I found what was to be my fate, and that the Indian who was before me and presented his gun was one of those who had just before fired. Two of my companions were taken with me in the same manner, the Indians assuring us we should not be hurt. But one in company, James Paul, who had a gun in order, made his escape and has since come into Wheeling. One of these Indians knew me, and was of the party by whom I was taken in the last war.

He came up and spoke to me calling me by my
Indian name, Mannuchothee, and upbraiding
me for coming to war against them.   I will
take a moment here to relate some particulars
of my first captivity and my life since.   I was
taken from New River in Virginia by the
Miamese, a nation called by us Picts, amongst
whom I lived six years, afterwards being sold
to a Delaware and by him put into the hands
of a trader.   I was carried amongst the
Shawanese, with whom I continued six years;
so that my whole time amongst these nations
was twelve years, that is, from the eighth to
the twentieth year of my age.   At the treaty
of Fort Pitt, in the fall preceding what is called
Dunmore's War, which if I am right, was in
the year 1773, I came in with the Shawanese
nation to the treaty, and meeting with some
of my relations at that place, was by them
solicited to relinquish the life of a savage,
which I did with some reluctance, this manner
of life having become natural to me, inasmuch
as I had scarcely known any other.   I en-
listed as a soldier in the continental army
at the commencement of the present war,
and served fifteen months.   Having been
properly discharged I have since married,

have a family and am in communion with the church.

To return, the party by whom we were made prisoners had taken some horses, and left them at the glades we had passed the day before. They had followed on our tracks from these glades, on our return to which we found the horses and rode. We were carried to Wachatomakak, a town of the Mingoes and Shawanese. I think it was on the third day we reached the town, which when we were approaching, the Indians in whose custody we were, began to look sour, having been kind to us before and given us a little meat and flour to eat, which they had found or taken from some of our men on their retreat. This town is small and we were told was about two miles distant from the main town to which they intended to carry us.

The inhabitants from this town came out with clubs and tomahawks, struck, beat and abused us greatly. One of my two companions they seized, and having stripped him naked, blacked him with coal and water. This was the sign of being burnt; the man seemed to surmise it, and shed tears. He asked me the meaning of his being blacked; but I was for-

bid by the enemy in their own language, to
tell him what was intended. In English, which
they spoke easily, having been often at Fort
Pitt, they assured him he was not to be hurt.
I know of no reason for making him the first
object of their cruelty unless it was that he
was the oldest.

A warrior had been sent to the great town
to acquaint them with our coming and prepare
them for the frolic; for on our coming to it, the
inhabitants came out with guns, clubs and
tomahawks. We were told that we had to run
to the council house, about three hundred
yards. The man that was blacked was about
twenty yards before us in running the gauntlet.
They made him their principal object, men,
women and children beating him, and those
who had guns firing loads of powder on him as
he ran naked, putting the muzzles of the guns
to his body, shouting, hallooing and beating
their drums in the meantime.

The unhappy man had reached the door of
the council house, beat and wounded in a manner shocking to the sight; for having arrived
before him we had it in our power to view the
spectacle—it was indeed the most horrid that
can be conceived. They had cut him with

their tomahawks, shot his body black, burnt it into holes with loads of powder blown into him; a large wadding had made a wound in his shoulder whence the blood gushed.

Agreeable to the declaration of the enemy, when he first set out he had reason to think himself secure when he had reached the door of the council house. This seemed to be his hope, for coming up with great struggling and endeavors, he laid hold of the door but was pulled back and drawn away by them; finding they intended no mercy, but putting him to death, he attempted several times to snatch or lay hold of some of their tomahawks, but being weak could not effect it. We saw him borne off, and they were a long time beating, wounding and pursuing and killing him.

That same evening I saw the dead body of this man close by the council house. It was mangled cruelly, and the blood mingled with the powder was rendered black. The same evening I saw him after he had been cut to pieces, and his limbs and head about two hundred yards on the outside of the town put on poles. That evening also I saw the bodies of three others in the same black and mangled condition; these I was told had been put to death the same day, and just before we had reached the town. Their bodies as they lay were black, bloody, burnt with powder. Two of these were Harrison * and young Crawford.† I knew the visage of Col. Harrison, and I saw his clothing and that of young Crawford at the town. They brought horses to me and asked if I knew them. I said they were Harrison and Crawford's; they said they were.

The third of these men I did not know, but believe to have been Col. M. Cleland, the third in command on the expedition. The next day the bodies of these men were dragged to the outside of the town and their carcases being given to the dogs, their limbs and heads were stuck upon poles.

---

* This was Col. Harrison, son-in-law to Col. Crawford, one of the first men in the Western country. He had been greatly active on many occasions in devising measures for the defence of the frontiers, and his character as a citizen in every way, then a young man, distinguished and respectable. He had been a magistrate under the jurisdiction of Virginia, and I believe a delegate to the Assembly of that State. I know no man with whose grave, sedate manners, prudent conduct, good sense and public spirit on all occasions I was more pleased.　　　　H. B.

† This was a son of Col. Crawford. I do not remember to have seen him, nor was I acquainted with his character before the expedition, but have since been informed universally, that he was a young man greatly and deservedly esteemed as a soldier and as a citizen.　　　　H. B.

My surviving companion shortly after we had reached the council house was sent to another town, and I presume, he was burnt or executed in the same manner.

In the evening the men assembled in the council house; this is a large building about fifty yards in length, and about twenty-five yards wide, and about sixteen feet in height, built of split poles covered with bark; their first object was to examine me, which they could do in their own language, inasmuch as I could speak the Miame, Shawanese and Delaware languages, which I had learned during my early captivity in the last war; I found I had not forgotten these languages, especially the two former, as well as my native tongue.

They began with interrogating me, concerning the situation of our country, what were our provisions? our numbers? the state of the war between us and Britain? I informed them Cornwallis had been taken, which next day, when Mathew Elliot with James Girty * came, he

---

* These men, Elliot and Girty, were inhabitants of the Western country, and since the commencement of the war, for some time professed an attachment to America, went off to the Indians. They are of that horrid brood called Refugees, and whom the devil has long since marked for his own property.

affirmed to be a lie, and the Indians seemed to give full credit to his declaration.

Hitherto I had been treated with some appearance of kindness, but now the enemy began to alter their behavior towards me. Girty had informed them, that when he asked me how I liked to live there, I had said that I intended to take the first opportunity to take a scalp and run off. It was, to be sure, very probable that if I had such intention, I would communicate it to him. Another man came to me and told me a story of his having lived on the south branch of Potomac in Virginia, and having three brothers there, he pretended he wanted to get away, but I suspected his design; nevertheless he reported that I had consented to go. In the mean time I was not tied, and could have escaped, but having nothing to put on my feet, I waited some time longer to provide for this.

I was invited every night to the war dance, which they usually continued until almost day. I could not comply with their desire, believing these things to be the service of the devil.

The council lasted fifteen days; fifty to one hundred warriors being usually in council, and sometimes more. Every warrior is admitted to these councils : but only the chiefs or head warriors have the privilege of speaking. The head warriors are accounted such from the number of scalps and prisoners they have taken.

The third day McKee* was in council, and afterwards was generally present. He spoke little, and did not ask any questions or speak to me at all. He lives about two miles out of town, has a house built of square logs with a shingle roof; he was dressed in gold laced clothes. I had seen him at the former town through which I passed.

I think it was on the last day of the council, save one, that a speech came from Detroit, brought by a warrior who had been counselling with the commanding officer at that place. The speech had been long expected, and was in answer to one some time before sent from the town to Detroit. It was in a belt of Wampum, and began with addressing them, " My children," and inquiring why they continue to take prisoners? Provisions are scarce ; when

---

* This man before the war was an Indian agent for the British. He was put on parole, broke it, went to the Indians and has since continued violently to incite them to make war against us.

5

prisoners are brought in we are obliged to
maintain them, and still some of them are running away and carrying tidings of our affairs.
When any of your people fall into the hands
of the rebels, they show no mercy; why then
should you take prisoners? Take no more
prisoners, my children, of any sort; man,
woman or child."

Two days after, a party of every nation that
was near being collected, it was determined on
to take no more prisoners of any sort. They
had held a large council, and the determination
was, that if it were possible they could find a
child of a span or three inches long, they would
show no mercy to it. At the conclusion of
the council it was agreed upon by all the tribes
present, viz.: the Tawaws, Chippawaws, the
Wyandots, the Mingoes, the Delawares, the
Shawanese, Munses, and a part of the Che-
rokees, that should any of the nations who
were not present take any prisoners, these would
rise against them, take away the prisoners and
put them to death.

In the course of these deliberations I understood what was said perfectly. They laid plans
against our settlements of Kentucky, the Falls,
and towards Wheeling. These it will be un-

necessary for me to mention in this narrative, more especially as the Indians finding me to have escaped, and knowing that I would not fail to communicate these designs, will be led to alter their resolutions.

There was one council held at which I was not present. The warriors had sent for me as usual, but the squaw with whom I lived would not suffer me to go, but hid me under a large quantity of skins. It may have been from an unwillingness that I should hear in council the determination with respect to me, that I should be burnt.

About this time, twelve men were brought in from Kentucky, three of whom were burnt on this day; the remainder were distributed to other towns, and all, as the Indians informed me, were burnt. This was after the speech came from Detroit.

On the day after, I saw an Indian who had just come into town, and who said that the prisoners he was bringing to be burnt, and who he said was a doctor, had made his escape from him. I knew this must have been Dr. Knight, who went as surgeon of the expedition. The Indian had a wound four inches long in his head, which he acknowledged the doctor had given him; he was cut to the skull. His story was that he had untied the doctor, being asked by him to do so, the doctor promising that he would not go away; that while he was employed in kindling the fire the doctor snatched up the gun had come behind and struck him; that he then made a stroke at the doctor with his knife, which he laid hold of, and his fingers were cut almost off, the knife being drawn through his hand; that he gave the doctor two stabs, one in the back, the other in the belly; said the doctor was a great, big, tall, strong man. Being now adopted in an Indian family, and having some confidence for my safety, I took the liberty to contradict this, and said that I knew the doctor, who was a weak, little man. The other warriors laughed immoderately, and did not seem to credit him.* At this time I was told that Col. Crawford was burnt, and they greatly exulted over it.

The day after the council I have mentioned, about forty warriors, accompanied by George Girty, came early in the morning round the

---

* It is well known that Mr. Slover mentioned these circumstances at his first coming into Wheeling, and before he could have known the relation of the doctor, for that this is an evidence of the truth of the doctor's account, and his own.   H. B.

house where I was. The squaws gave me up, I was sitting before the door of the house; they put a rope round my neck, tied my arms behind my back, stripped me naked, and blacked me in the usual manner. George Girty, as soon as I was tied, d—d me, and said that I now should get what I had deserved many years. I was led away to a town distant about five miles, to which a messenger had been despatched to desire them to prepare to receive me.

Arriving at this town, I was beaten with clubs and the pipe ends of their tomahawks, and was kept for some time tied to a tree before a house door. In the meanwhile the inhabitants set out to another town about two miles distant, where I was to be burnt, and where I arrived about three o'clock in the afternoon.

Here also was a council house, part of it covered and part of it without a roof. In the part of it where no cover was, but only sides built up, there stood a post about sixteen feet in height, and in the middle of the house around the post, there were three piles of wood built about three feet high and four feet from the post.

Being brought to the post my arms were tied behind me, and the thong or cord with which they were bound was fastened to the post; a rope also was put about my neck, and tied to the post about four feet above my head. During the time they were tying me, piles of wood were kindled and began to flame.

Death by burning, which appeared to be now my fate, I had resolved to sustain with patience. The divine grace of God had made it less alarming to me; for on my way this day I had been greatly exercised in regard to my latter end. I knew myself to have been a regular member of the church, and to have sought repentance for my sins; but though I had often heard of the faith of assurance, had known nothing of it; but early this day, instantaneously by a change wrought upon me sudden and perceivable as lightning, an assurance of my peace made with God, sprung up in mind. The following words were the subject of my meditation —" In peace thou shalt see God. Fear not those who can kill the body. In peace shalt thou depart." I was on this occasion by a confidence in mind not to be resisted, fully assured of my salvation. This being the case I was willing, satisfied and glad to die.

I was tied to the post, as I have already said, and the flame was now kindled. The day was clear, not a cloud to be seen. If there were clouds low in the horizon, the sides of the house prevented me from seeing them, but I heard no thunder, or observed any sign of approaching rain; just as the fire of one pile began to blaze, the wind rose, from the time they began to kindle the fire and to tie me to the post, until the wind began to blow, was about fifteen minutes. The wind blew a hurricane, and the rain followed in less than three minutes. The rain fell violent; and the fire, though it began to blaze considerably, was instantly extinguished. The rain lasted about a quarter of an hour.

When it was over the savages stood amazed, and were a long time silent. At last one said, we will let him alone till morning, and take a whole day's frolic in burning him. The sun at this time was about three hours high. It was agreed upon, and the rope about my neck was untied, and making me sit down, they began to dance round me. They continued dancing in this manner until eleven o'clock at night; in the mean time, beating,

kicking and wounding me with their tomahawks and clubs.*

At last one of the warriors, the Half Moon,
asked me if I was sleepy? I answered, yes,
The head warrior then chose out three warriors to take care of me. I was taken to a
block house; my arms were tied until the cord
was hid in the flesh, they were tied in two
places, round the wrist and above the elbows.
A rope was fastened about my neck and tied
to a beam of the house, but permitting me to
lie down on a board. The three warriors were
constantly harassing and troubling me, saying,
" How will you like to eat fire to morrow—you
will kill no more Indians now." I was in
expectation of their going to sleep, when at
length, about an hour before daybreak, two
laid down, the third smoked a pipe, talked to
me and asked the same painful questions.
About half an hour after, he also laid down;
I heard him begin to snore. Instantly I went
to work, and as my arms were perfectly dead
with the cord, I laid myself down upon my

---

* I observed marks on the man when I saw him, which
was eight or ten days after he came in, particularly a wound
above his right eyebrow, which he had received with the
pipe end of a tomahawk; but his back and body generally
had been injured.   H. B.

right arm which was behind my back, and keeping it fast with my fingers, which had still some life and strength, I slipped the cord from my left arm over my elbow and my wrist. One of the warriors now got up and stirred the fire. I was apprehensive that I should be examined, and thought it was over with me, but my hopes revived when now he lay down again. I then attempted to unloose the rope about my neck; tried to gnaw it, but it was in vain, as it was as thick as my thumb and as hard as iron, being made of a buffalo hide. I wrought with it a long time, gave it out, and could see no relief. At this time I saw daybreak and heard the cock crow. I made a second attempt, almost without hope, pulling the rope by putting my fingers between my neck and it, and to my great surprise it came easily untied. It was a noose with two or three knots tied over it.

I slipped over the warriors as they lay, and having got out of the house, looked back to see if there was any disturbance. I then ran through the town into a corn field; in my way I saw a squaw with four or five children lying asleep under a tree. Going in a different way into the field, I untied my arm, which was

6

greatly swollen and turned black. Having observed a number of horses in the glade as I ran through it, I went back to catch one, and on my way found a piece of an old rug or quilt hanging on a fence, which I took with me. Having caught the horse, the rope with which I had been tied served for a halter, I rode off. The horse was strong and swift, and the woods being open and the country level, about ten o'clock that day I crossed the Scioto river at a place, by computation, fifty full miles from the town. I had rode about twenty-five miles on this side of the Scioto by three o'clock in the afternoon, when the horse began to fail, and could no longer go on a trot. I instantly left him, and on foot, ran about twenty miles farther that day, making in the whole the distance of near one hundred miles. In the evening I heard hallooing behind me, and for this reason did not halt until about ten o'clock at night, when I sat down, was extremely sick and vomited; but when the moon rose, which might have been about two hours after, I went on and traveled until day.

During the night I had a path, but in the morning judged it prudent to forsake the path and take a ridge for the distance of fifteen miles, in a line at right angles to my course, putting back as I went along, with a stick, the weeds which I had bent, lest I should be tracked by the enemy. I lay the next night on the waters of Muskingum; the nettles had been troublesome to me after my crossing the Scioto, having nothing to defend myself but the piece of a rug which I had found and which while I rode I used under me by way of a saddle; the briars and thorns were now painful to, and prevented me from traveling in the night until the moon appeared. In the meantime I was prevented from sleeping by the mosquitoes, for even in the day I was under the necessity of traveling with a handfull of bushes to brush them from my body.

The second night I reached Cushakim, next day came to Newcomer's town, where I got about seven raspberries, which were the first thing I ate from the morning on which the Indians had taken me to burn me until this time, which was now about three o'clock the fourth day. I felt hunger very little, but was extremely weak. I swam Muskingum river at Oldcomer's town, the river being two hundred yards wide; having reached the bank, I sat down, looked back and thought I had a start of the Indians if any should pursue. That evening I traveled about five miles; next day came to Stillwater, a small river, in a branch of which I got two small crawfish to eat. Next night I lay within five miles of Wheeling, but had not slept a wink during this whole time, being rendered impossible by the mosquitoes, which it was my constant employment to brush away. Next day came to Wheeling, and saw a man on the island in the Ohio opposite to that post, and calling to him and asking for particular persons who had been on the expedition, and telling him I was Slover, at length, with great difficulty, he was persuaded to come over and bring me across in his canoe.*

---

* It has been said that the putting to death the Moravian Indians has been the cause of the cruelties practised on the prisoners taken at Sandusky. But though this has been made an excuse by the refugees amongst the savages, and by the British, yet it must be well known that it has been the custom of the savages at all times. I have it from Col. John Campbell, who is lately from Chamblee, where he has been in confinement a long time, and was taken on the Ohio some years ago, that two men who were taken with him were put to death at the Shawanese towns in the same manner in which Harrison was afterwards executed, viz.: by blowing powder into their bodies. A large load blown

At the same time, though I would strike away this excuse which is urged for the savages, I am far from approving the Moravian slaughter. Doubtless the existence of that body of people in our neighborhood, was of disadvantage, as they were under the necessity of receiving and refusing the Sandusky savages as they came to war, and as they returned, and as no doubt some amongst them communicated intelligence of any expedition on foot against the enemy. I am also disposed to believe, that the greater part of the men put to death were warriors; this appears from the testimony of one against another, from the confession of many, from their singing the war song when ordered out to be tomahawked, from the cut and painting of their hair, and from other circumstances. The greater part of the Moravian men who were really peaceable or well affected to us, having

---

into the body of one of these men, reaching his kidneys, the pain throwing him into rage and madness, the savages were uncommonly diverted with the violence of his exclamation and gestures; boys of the town, particularly, following him, and considering it as excellent sport. In the evening his head was cut off and an end put to his misery. Col. Campbell himself was led out to make sport of the same kind, but was saved by the interposition, I think, of Elliot.

been carried off the fall before, and still detained at Sandusky.

But the putting to death the women and children, who sang hymns at their execution, must be considered as unjustifiable, inexcusable homicide; and the Colonel who commanded the party, and who is said perseveringly, contrary to the remonstrances of officers present, to have enjoined the perpetration of the act, has not yet been called to an account, is a disgrace to the State of Pennsylvania.

H. BRACKINRIDGE.

Mr. Baily :

With the narrative enclosed, I subjoin some observations with regard to the animals, vulgarly called Indians. It is not my intention to write any labored essay; for at so great a distance from the city, and so long unaccustomed to write, I have scarcely resolution to put pen to paper. Having an opportunity to know something of the character of this race of men, from the deeds they perpetrate daily round me, I think proper to say something on the subject. Indeed, several years ago, and before I left your city, I had thought different from some others with respect to the right of soil, and the propriety of forming treaties and making peace with them.

In the United States Magazine in the year 1777, I published a dissertation denying them to have a right in the soil. I perceive a writer in your very elegant and useful paper, has taken up the same subject, under the signature of "Caractacus," and unanswerably shown, that their claim to the extensive countries of America, is wild and inadmissible. I will take the liberty in this place, to pursue this subject a little.

On what is their claim founded? — Occupancy. A wild Indian with his skin painted red, and a feather through his nose, has set his foot on the broad continent of North and South America; a second wild Indian with his ears cut in ringlets, or his nose slit like a swine or a malefactor, also sets his foot on the same extensive tract of soil. Let the first Indian make a talk to his brother, and bid him take his foot off the continent, for he being first upon it, had occupied the whole, to kill buffaloes, and tall elks with long horns. This claim in the reasoning of some men would be just, and the second savage ought to depart in his canoe, and seek a continent where no prior occupant claimed the soil. Is this claim of occupancy of a very early date? When Noah's three sons, Shem, Ham, and Japhet, went out to the three quarters of the old world, Ham to Africa, Shem to Asia, Japhet to Europe, did each claim a quarter of the world for his residence? Suppose Ham to have spent his time fishing or gathering oysters in the Red Sea, never once stretching his leg in a long walk to see his vast dominions, from the mouth of the Nile, across the mountains of Ethiopia and the river Niger to the Cape of Good Hope, where the Hottentots, a cleanly people, now stay; or supposing him, like a Scots pedlar, to have traveled over many thousand leagues of that country; would this give him a right to the soil? In the opinion of some men it would establish an exclusive right. Let a man in more modern times take a journey or voyage like Patrick Kennedy and others to the heads of the

Mississippi or Missouri rivers, would he gain a right ever after to exclude all persons from drinking the waters of these streams ? Might not a second Adam make a talk to them and say, is the whole of this water necessary to allay your thirst, and may I also drink of it ?

The whole of this earth was given to man, and all descendants of Adam have a right to share it equally. There is no right of primogeniture in the laws of nature and of nations. There is reason that a tall man, such as the chaplain in the American army we call the High Priest, should have a large spot of ground to stretch himself upon ; or that a man with a big belly, like a goodly alderman of London, should have a larger garden to produce beans and cabbage for his appetite, but that an agile, nimble runner, like an Indian called the Big Cat, at Fort Pitt, should have more than his neighbors, because he has traveled a great space, I can see no reason.

I have conversed with some persons and found their mistakes on this subject, to arise from a view of claims by individuals in a state of society, from holding a greater proportion

of the soil than others; but this is according
to the laws to which they have consented; an
individual holding one acre, cannot encroach
on him who has a thousand, because he is
bound by the law which secures property in
this unequal manner. This is the municipal
law of the state under which he lives. The
member of a distant society is not excluded
by the laws from a right to the soil. He
claims under the general law of nature, which
gives a right, equally to all, to so much of the
soil as is necessary for subsistence. Should a
German from the closely peopled country
of the Rhine, come into Pennsylvania, more
thinly peopled, he would be justifiable in demanding a settlement, though his personal
force would not be sufficient to effect it. It
may be said that the cultivation or melioration
of the earth, gives a property in it. No—if
an individual has engrossed more than is
necessary to produce grain for him to live
upon, his useless gardens, fields and pleasure
walks, may be seized upon by the person
who, not finding convenient ground elsewhere,
choose to till them for his support.

It is a usual way of destroying an opinion
by pursuing it to its consequence. In the

present case we may say, that if the visiting one acre of ground could give a right to it, the visiting of a million would give a right on the same principle; and thus a few surly ill natured men, might in the earlier ages have excluded half the human race from a settlement, or should any have fixed themselves on a territory, visited before they had set a foot on it, they must be considered as invaders of the rights of others.

It is said that an individual, building a house or fabricating a machine has an exclusive rights to it, and why not those who improve the earth ? I would say, should man build houses on a greater part of the soil, than falls to his share, I would, in a state of nature, take away a proportion of the soil and the houses from him, but a machine or any work of art, does not lessen the means of subsistence to the human race, which an extensive occupation of the soil does.

Claims founded on the first discovery of soil are futile. When gold, jewels, manufactures, or any work of men's hands is lost, the finder is entitled to some reward, that is, he has some claims on the thing found, for a share of it.

When by industry or the exercise of genius, something unusual is invented in medicine or in other matters, the author doubtless has a claim to an exclusive profit by it, but who will say the soil is lost, or that any one can found a claim by discovering it.   The earth with its woods and rivers still exist, and the only advantage I would allow to any individual for having cast his eye first on any particular part of it, is the privilege of making the first choice of situation.   I would think the man a fool and unjust, who would exclude me from drinking the waters of the Mississippi river, because he had first seen it.   He would be equally so who would exclude me from settling in the country west of the Ohio, because in chasing a buffalo he had been first over it.

The idea of an exclusive right to the soil in the natives had its origin in the policy of the first discoverers, the kings of Europe. Should they deny the right of the natives from their first treading on the continent, they would take away the right of discovery in themselves, by sailing on the coast.   As the vestige of the moccasin in one case gave a right, so the cruise in the other was the foundation of a claim.

Those who under these kings, derived grants were led to countenance the idea, for otherwise why should kings grant or they hold extensive tracts of country. Men become enslaved to an opinion that has been long entertained. Hence it is that many wise and good men will talk of the right of savages to immense tracts of soil.

What use do these ring, streaked, spotted and speckled cattle make of the soil? Do they till it? Revelation said to man, "Thou shalt till the ground." This alone is human life. It is favorable to population, to science, to the information of a human mind in the worship of God. Warburton has well said, that before you can make an Indian a christian you must teach him agriculture and reduce him to a civilized life. To live by tilling is *more bumano*, by hunting is *more best arum.* I would as soon admit a right in the buffalo to grant lands, as in Killbuck, the Big Cat, the Big Dog, or any of the ragged wretches that are called chiefs and sachems. What would you think of going to a big lick or place where the beasts collect to lick saline nitrous earth and water, and addressing yourself to a great buffalo to grant you land? It is true he could not make the mark of the stone or the mountain reindeer, but he could set his cloven foot to the instrument like the great Ottomon, the father of the Turks, when he put his signature to an instrument, he put his large hand and spreading fingers in the ink and set his mark to the parchment. To see how far the folly of some would go, I had once a thought of supplicating some of the great elks or buffaloes that run through the woods, to make me a grant of a hundred thousand acres of land and prove he had brushed the weeds with his tail, and run fifty miles.

I wonder if Congress or the different States would recognize the claim? I am so far from thinking the Indians have a right to the soil, that not having made a better use of it for many hundred years, I conceive they have forfeited all pretence to claim, and ought to be driven from it.

With regard to forming treaties or making peace with this race, there are many ideas:

They have the shapes of men and may be of the human species, but certainly in their present state they approach nearer the character of Devils; take an Indian, is there any faith in him? Can you bind him by favors? Can you trust his word or confide in his promise? When he makes war upon you, when he takes you prisoner and has you in his power will he spare you? In this he departs from the law of nature, by which, according to baron Montesquieu and every other man who thinks on the subject, it is unjustifiable to take away the life of him who submits; the conqueror in doing otherwise becomes a murderer, who ought to be put to death. On this principle are not the whole Indian nations murderers?

Many of them may have not had an opportunity of putting prisoners to death, but the sentiment which they entertain leads them invariably to this when they have it in their power or judge it expedient; these principles constitute them murderers, and they ought to be prevented from carrying them into execution, as we would prevent a common homicide, who should be mad enough to conceive himself justifiable in killing men.

The tortures which they exercise on the bodies of their prisoners, justify extermination. Gelo of Syria made war on the Carthaginians because they oftentimes burnt human victims, and made peace with them on conditions they would cease from this unnatural and cruel practice.　If we could have any faith in the promises they make we could suffer them to live, provided they would only make war amongst themselves, and abandon their hiding or lurking on the pathways of our citizens, emigrating unarmed and defenceless inhabitants; and murdering men, women and children in a defenceless situation; and on their ceasing in the meantime to raise arms no more among the American Citizens.

MISS COLESON'S NARRATIVE

OF HER CAPTIVITY

AMONG THE SIOUX INDIANS!

"Her child, an infant a few months old, she managed to conceal in her clothing, but on arriving at the place where the women were, it was discovered."—*See Page* 54

MISS COLESON'S NARRATIVE

OF HER CAPTIVITY

AMONG THE SIOUX INDIANS!

AN INTERESTING AND REMARKABLE ACCOUNT

OF THE

TERRIBLE SUFFERINGS

AND

PROVIDENTIAL ESCAPE

OF

MISS ANN COLESON,

A VICTIM OF THE LATE INDIAN OUTRAGES IN MINNESOTA.

PHILADELPHIA:
PUBLISHED BY BARCLAY & CO.
No. 602 ARCH STREET.
1864.

THRILLING ADVENTURES

OF

MISS ANN COLESON,

AMONG THE INDIANS.

ON THE night of the 12th of January, 1863, the dwelling of the widow Coleson, near New Ulm, in Minnesota, was attacked by a straggling party of Sioux Indians, under their Chief, White Eagle, a warrior of some renown. This dwelling was built in primitive style, of logs, in the form of a double cabin, of which one room was tenanted by Mrs. Coleson and her family of four persons, two sons and two daughters, all grown to maturity; while the other was occupied by a hunter named Marts, his wife and three children.

The hour was twelve o'clock at night. One of the daughters was still busily engaged at the loom, and the other was spinning flax. Both young men had retired to rest, so had the children of Mrs. Marts, though that lady and Mrs. Coleson were sitting up waiting the return of Marts, and wondering why he did not come.

In these new settlements, it is not unusual for families, to be supplied with food for months from the forest and the river. Thus the skill of the husband and father is brought into daily requisition. His return at nightfall laden with the spoils of the chase, is anticipated with the fondest anxiety by the wife and her little ones. Should he be un-avoidably detained by accidents, wandering out of the way, or other misfortunes, she experiences all the tortures of apprehension and sus-pense; goes to the door and looks out, listening every few minutes, neither can she banish the thought that something dreadful has happened, until re-assured by his well known step and welcome voice.

On the evening in question, the darkness of the night, the lateness of the hour, the unusual absence of Marts, and perhaps a sense of impending danger, all conspired to give earnestness and tone to the conversation of the two elderly women as they sat cowering over the fire, whose light and warmth irradiated the entire apartment.

"There's something going to happen, I know very well," said Mrs. Coleson, her voice falling to a mysterious whisper, "and if it is not death, never you believe me again; John says it is nothing, but I am older than John."

"You speak of the dog," said Mrs. Marts.

"Yes, the dog; you heard him as well as myself, sighing and moaning like a human creature in pain, and all night long, too—not a regular howl, but a cry of agony—I couldn't sleep for it, you couldn't sleep for it, Ann and Sally couldn't sleep for it."

"Hark! what's that?" interrupted Mrs. Marts.

Both women listened.

"Owls," said Mrs. Coleson.

"That isn't their usual manner of hooting, is it?" inquired Mrs. Marts, "I will go to the door and listen, maybe I'll hear something of Marts."

"Don't you open the door!" exclaimed Mrs. Coleson. "You don't know who or what you may be letting in."

"Why, what do you mean?" said Mrs. Marts, eyeing her companion with a sort of amazed curiosity.

"Just what I say, don't you open that door!"

"There's somebody," and Mrs. Marts held up her finger in a listening attitude.

"The horses, I guess," answered Mrs. Coleson.

These animals were enclosed as usual in a pond near the house, and by repeated snorting and galloping announced the presence of some object of terror.

"You had better call John," said Mrs. Marts.

"I will," and Mrs. Coleson ascended to the loft, where her sons slept. John the elder was wide awake and had been for some time. He had often been upon the point of calling his brother Thomas, but had been as often restrained by the fear of incurring ridicule, and the reproach of timidity, in that neighborhood, an unpardonable blemish on the character of a man. From the commencement of the alarming symptons, he had felt convinced that mischief was brewing. Rising at once, when his mother appeared, the movement awakened Thomas, who demanded "What was the matter?" Before either had time to reply, hasty steps were heard in the yard, and quickly afterwards several raps at the door accompanied by a demand for admittance in a voice evidently intended to simulate that of Marts.

By this time both Mrs. Coleson and her sons had reached the basement, while Mrs. Marts, thinking only of her husband, hastily arose and advanced to withdraw the bar, which secured the door, when Mrs. Coleson, who had lived long upon the frontier and probably had detected the Indian tone in the words just uttered, sprang forward and ordered Mrs. Marts not to admit them, declaring that they were Indians.

" Boys, to your guns" she cried, with the look and manner of a heroine.

The young men immediately sprung to their arms, which were always charged, prepared to repel an enemy.

The Indians finding that their true character had been discovered, began to thunder at the door with great violence, but a single shot from a loop-hole compelled them to shift the attack to some less exposed point and unfortunately they discovered the back door of the cabin, which was much less securely guarded and which communicated with the apartment where the girls were at work   The rifles of the brothers could not be brought to bear upon all points at once.   By means of rails taken from the yard fence, the door was broken open, and the two girls were at the mercy of the savages.   Ann was immediately secured, stripped entirely naked, and subjected to the most horrible of personal outrages; but Sally, seeing the fate of her sister, determined to die rather than surrender.   Seizing a large carving knife she had been using in the loom, she defended herself desperately, and stabbed one of the Indians to the heart, before she was tomahawked.

Presently the crackling of flames was heard, accompanied by a triumphant yell from the Indians, announcing that they had set fire to that division of the house which had been occupied by the daughters, and of which they held undisputed possession.

The fire was quickly communicated to the rest of the building, and it became necessary either to abandon it or perish in the flames.   In the one case there was a bare possibility that some might escape; in the other, death would be inevitable.   The rapid approach of the fire allowed but little time for consideration.   Even then the flames had made a breach, and some of the Indians were preparing to enter.   The door was thrown open, and all rushed out; Mrs. Coleson, guarded by her eldest son, attempted to cross the fence at one place, while the other son, carrying the two eldest children, hurried off in another direction, leaving Mrs. Marts with her infant, to follow as she best could.

In their eagerness to secure the provisions and valuables belonging to the house, the Indians at first paid little attention to their escape, and Mrs. Coleson had reached the stile and was crossing over, when she was severely wounded in several places by rifle balls, she fell shrieking in agony; her son, paralysed by grief and horror, stooped over to assist her, when he was instantly seized upon from behind, and made a prisoner. The other young man succeeded in reaching the fence unhurt, but in the act of passing was vigorously assailed by several Indians, who, throwing down their guns rushed upon him with their tomahawks. He made a gallant defence, firing upon the enemy as they pproached, and then wielding the butt of his rifle with a fury, that drew their whole attention upon himself, he gave Mrs. Marts and her children an opportunity of effecting their escape. However, he was soon overpowered by numbers, wounded both in the head and breast, and taken prisoner.

Mrs. Marts might have escaped to a place of safety with her children, had she taken advantage of the darkness and pre-occupation of the enemy and fled, but instead of that the terrified woman ran around the house wringing her hands, and shrieking in frantic despair. This was followed by a faint moan. One of the savages had sunk his tomahawk in her brain. She was then scalped, her body mutilated in a shocking manner, and then thrown warm and bleeding into the flames.

The infant as it fell from her arms, was seized by a huge wolf dog, and actually devoured alive. One of the other children, a boy about three years old, screamed and wept at the dreadful fate of the baby. This irritated the savages. One of them took him by the heels, dashed him against a tree, stabbed and scalped him, then threw him also into the fire. The other child, a girl, was too frightened even to weep, hence she was suffered to live.

Thus of two happy families of five persons each, only four individuals escaped the slaughter, and these were exposed to all the horrors and sufferings of captivity in mid-winter.

The cold was intense, the snow two feet upon a level; the prisoners thinly clad. The young men in the hurry of the moment, when first attacked, had forgotten to put on their coats and since then they had not had the opportunity; now with no protection but their shirts and trowsers, the cutting north wind seemed to peirce their very bones, still, as it congealed the blood around their wounds, and thus prevented the bleeding, it proved a real advantage to them. Their own sufferings were forgotten in witnessing the dreadful condition of their sister, and being denied the privilege of assisting her. The Chief, White Eagle, in an unusual fit of amiability allowed her the use of some old garments, which were only serviceable as being better than none.

The captives were hurried off in a northerly direction and soon reached a dense forest of pines, where the Indians halted to arrange and tie up their plunder. While they were busy about this John Coleson counted them, and the whole number amounted to forty eight, including two white men, who were with them painted and plumed as they were; several of the Indians could speak English and the brothers knew some of them very well; having often seen them going up and down the rivers. The greater number were Sioux, though there were individuals belonging to other tribes.

After stopping, perhaps fifteen minutes, they resumed their journey, and were soon joined by other parties of Indians, some on foot, others on horseback, but all loaded with plunder and accompanied by prisoners of all ages and conditions. The savages wore snow-shoes, and travelled rapidly, driving their captives before them like so many cattle. When one began to lag behind the others, they whipped and scourged the naked flesh of the sufferer to hasten his or her speed. When one gave out entirely, and blows were powerless to make him or her go farther, they would sear the tenderest parts of the victim's body with lighted pine torches, tear out the entrails and pluck off the scalp. In some instances they cut of the breasts of women, roasted the flesh and compelled the survivors to partake of it. Thus, the number of captives gradually diminished, and before morning all the more delicate women and many of the children had perished.

An hour before sunrise they halted for breakfast, and kindled a fire. The captives wanted to approach in order to warm their stiffened limbs; this the Indians, in mere wantoness of cruelty, forbade—hence the poor tired creatures were obliged to keep in constant motion to prevent their being frozen. Some of the captives got a morsel or two to eat, but by far the greater number received nothing, though suffering the keenest pangs of hunger. Here the Indians appeared to hold a council, and after it closed, they broke up into parties of two or three, and went off in different directions, each one appropriating to himself such captives as he claimed. This arrangement was a great grievance to the unhappy prisoners, as the dearest friends, who might have found some consolation in sharing each other's sorrows and knowing each other's fate, were thus separated, perhaps forever. Ann Coleson parted from her brothers with many tears. They, with their captors, went off towards the Great Missouri, while hers took the direction of the Northern Lakes. She, and a little girl, named Mary Ellis, whose parents had both been slain, were accompanied by two Indians and a Canadian half-breed, who led them to a place in the woods where three horses were picketed; each of the Indians mounted and took a prisoner behind him—the Canadian mounted the third horse, and started in the lead. They soon came to a river, which was frozen over, and they crossed on the ice; the little girl soon began to cry with hunger and excessive cold, when the Indian she rode with tomahawked and scalped her, leaving the body in the path to be devoured by the wolves.

Ann Coleson was thus left alone with her tormentors, but though suffering excessively, she feared to make any complaint. At length her

Indian master gave her a pair of leggins, lined with fur, and moccasins for the protection of her feet; she also received a small portion of dried deer's flesh, and a spoonful of whisky, which in her exhausted condition was exceedingly palatable and nourishing.

They travelled all day very hard, and that night arrived at a large camp, covered with bark, which by appearance might hold one hundred men; they took her, however, about three hundred yards from the camp, into a large, dark cave—bound her arms, spread a bed of buffalo and wolf skins, and laid down, one on each side of her.

The next morning they were joined by numbers of their former party, who had only separated from them and gone off in another direction in order to mislead and baffle pursuit, should one be instituted. They had many prisoners with them, some of whom it seemed had been condemned to the fiery torture, and painted black; others were manacled hand and foot, and all bore the marks of extreme hard usage. Ann Coleson looked in vain for her brothers, but though she recognized the Indians by whom they were captured, she saw nothing of them. Had they been exchanged for others? Or had they given out and been left on the road? This seemed most probable, and deeply as she felt their loss, her sorrow was modified by a feeling of satisfaction that they were beyond the reach of farther trouble.

This day they proceeded amid dreadful storms of snow and occasional torrents of rain, which drenched them to the skin, through a barren and desolate country, where it was impossible, with the wet moss and green brushwood, to kindle a fire. The Indians marched on with stoical indifference, mindless alike of wind or weather. Sometime through the day they killed a deer, which was cut up and eaten raw; the heart, warm and bleeding, was given to Ann—hunger is not fastidious, she devoured a small portion, and concealed the rest about her person till some future time.

She soon discovered that the savages were making preparations for another plundering expedition. Spies were sent out to discover whether any white men were in the neighborhood. After a short absence they returned with intelligence that they had seen six log houses, about twelve miles distant, on the east side of the river that communicates with Rainy Lake. All was now warlike preparation; the guns, knives and spears were carefully examined, and as they learned that the nature of the ground would render it easy to advance unperceived, it was determined to steal upon their victims in this manner. This plan was executed with the nicest exactness, and nothing could present a more dreadful view of human nature in its unenlightened state, than the perfect unanimity of purpose which pervaded the whole body of Indians on this horrid occasion, although at other times they were greatly at variance. Each man first painted his target, some with a representation of the sun, others of the moon, and several with the pictures of birds and beasts of prey, or of imaginary beings, which they affirmed to be the inhabitants of the elements, upon whose assistance they relied for success in their enterprise. They then moved with the utmost stealth in the direction of the houses, taking care not to cross any of the hills which concealed their approach. It was a miserable circumstance that the poor settlers had taken up their abode in such ground, that their enemies, without being observed, formed an ambuscade not two hundred yards distant, and lay for some time watching and marking their victims. Here they left their prisoners, all bound to trees, with gags in their mouths to prevent their making any noise or giving the alarm, and here they made their last preparations for the attack. The Indians tied up their hair in a knot, behind, lest it should be blown in their eyes; painted their faces black and red, which gave them a most hideous aspect; deliberately tucked up the sleeves of their jackets close under the armpits, and pulled off their moccasins; while some, still more eager to render themselves light for running, threw off their jackets, and stood with their weapons ready in their hands, quite naked, except their breech clothes.

It was near one o'clock in the morning when all their arrangements were completed. The settlers were all quietly sleeping, unconscious that danger was so near, when the Indians uttered a tremendous whoop and simultaneously rushed from their concealment. In an instant the unfortunate wretches, men women and children, were aroused. The men sprang for their fire arms, the women to barricade the doors, while others ran out and attempted to escape. The Indians however, had completely surrounded them; many were murdered in cold blood, and all the dwellings were set on fire.

These people were all Germans, against whom the savages had conceived a particular spite. One girl, about sixteen years of age, ran from the burning house of her parents, and came directly to the tree where Ann Coleson was bound; she was pursued by two Indians, one of whom stuck a spear in her side; she fell at Ann's feet, and clasped her ankles so tightly, that it was with difficulty she could extricate herself from the dying sufferers grasp. Notwithstanding the danger to herself, Ann solicited very hard for her life, but the murderers made no reply until they had both stuck their spears through her body, and transfixed her to the ground; they then looked Ann sternly in the face, and commanded her to be silent under the penalty of being treated in the same manner, while they laughed at and jeered the poor wretch, who was shrieking in agony and moving and twisting about their spears like a tortured worm.

Shocked and grieved beyond measure, Ann implored her master, who now came up, to dispatch the poor victim and end her misery, since she was so severely wounded that recovery would be impossible.

The wretched creature seemed to understand the purport of her words; she raised her eyes, and said something in German. Even in this most miserable state, the love of life was predominant; for though this might justly be called the most merciful act that could be done for the poor creature, it seemed to be unwelcome. Exhausted as she was by pain and loss of blood, she made several efforts to ward off the friendly blow; at last an Indian, with his spear pierced her through the heart, and she expired.

After this inhuman butchery, the Indians again separated, different parties going off in different directions; some professedly to hunt, the others to plunder and devastate the outside settlements. They evidently feared to come in contact with the United States troops—their chief aim and great delight being to surprise and butcher some frontier family, pick off some careless hunter, or kidnap women and children. They seemed also excessively afraid of the escape or recovery of their prisoners, and hence hurried them away by long and painful marches to their remotest towns.

Of the incidents connected with this long and wearisome journey, Ann Coleson gives a graphic and interesting description. Their party consisted of five persons, three Indians, herself and a captive boy. The want of forage, probably, or perhaps some other reason, had caused them to leave all the horses behind.

"They put us in harness," says Miss Coleson, in her Journal, meaning herself and the boy, whose name was Frank Scott.

"They put us in harness, with a broad leather strap passing over the breast and shoulders, to which a strong rope was attached, and thus we could drag a load, while our arms were at liberty. Among all the Indian tribes the females are expected to perform the drudgery, hence they had no mercy upon me, and not being accustomed to such work or such traveling, the sledge I was compelled to draw with the weight of plunder upon it, caused me to suffer intolerable fatigue. They gave me a pair of snow shoes, but not being accustomed to their use, which can only be acquired by a severe apprenticeship, they proved an encumbrance rather than otherwise.

"The Indians selected for their route the frozen surface of a river, the name of which I never learned. The snow shoes were heavy, and soon became thickly clogged with ice, there being much water between the surface of the river and the snow, which froze immediately; it was necessary to be provided with short sticks for beating this off. Before us was one uniform white expanse of snow, on each side a thick impenetrable forest. With our utmost exertions we could only proceed at the rate of two miles in an hour and a half; the Indians grumbled at this, and threatened all manner of terrible things, but upon finding that I really did my best, and could not possibly travel with greater speed, they considerately lightened my load, by removing several articles, which they buried in the snow.

" I shall never forget the sense of relief which came over me, when a halt for the night was ordered; such utter, utter weariness I had never before experienced. The poor boy, my fellow captive, was no better off; he was an invalid, suffering from disease of the heart, and altogether unable to endure such wearying toil. I wished to sympathize and converse with him, but the Indians forbade it; we were watched and guarded with the utmost jealousy—each look or word they interpreted to be significant of some plan to escape.

" Our resting place for the night was a small log hut, which stood on the river bank, and had probably at some past period been occupied by a party of hunters. The Indians had become much kinder in their manner towards us, not only allowing us a tolerable meal of roasted meat, but suffering us to sit by the fire, which was the greatest of all comforts. The fire-place ran along the entire end of the building, and was filled with enormous logs, the one at the back of the hearth being so heavy as to require the strength of two or three men, with the aid of levers, to bring it in; over this fire the moccassins and leggins of the whole party were hung to dry. To beds, and all other comforts except what fire could bestow, we had bidden adieu—but a pile of skins lay in one corner, and wrapped in one of these I slept soundly on the floor.

" The next day was a journey of twelve miles; snow had fallen in the night, and as it still lay soft, our progress was even made more difficult than before, if that were possible. At every step my feet felt as if chained to the ground, by ice and clotted snow, and as the shores of the river widened the feeling of disappointment was added to our other troubles: the point on which our eyes were wistfully fixed, appeared, after an hour's hard toiling, scarce nearer than before. Headland seemed separated from headland by interminable space, and we looked, oh, how long and vainly for the end.

" The boy, Frank, fell into an air-hole, up to his middle, where he hung, supporting himself by the arms, until he could be pulled out.— Unfortunately, against this danger no precaution could be of any avail, and we were obliged to take our chance for a ducking or a drowning; the Indians ungenerously compelled us to go first, and in this they were probably influenced quite as much by the love of ease as a sense of danger; for as the first one had to make the way upon the untrodden snow, and upon the large track of his or her snow-shoes those who followed found comparatively firm footing.

"The Indians prescribed our course according to their notions of the safety of the ice, which being founded on their recollected knowledge of the river, was but poor guidance—while many and circuitous was the paths we had to make in consequence. During the afternoon a snow storm came on, beating directly in our faces; it blew a hurricane; we were unable to see each other at a greater distance than ten yards, and the drift made the surface of the snow through which we were toiling, appear like an agitated sea. Wheeled round every now and then by the wind, the cloud which enveloped us was so strong that it produced a sense of suffocation. Even the Indians admitted that it was impossible to proceed; the forest was near, and there we took refuge, turning our shoulders to the blast, and preparing to bivouac for the night.

"For a wonder, the Indians went to work themselves; with their hatchets, they soon felled a good sized maple tree, while Frank and myself, with large pieces of bark ripped from the fallen tree, cleared of snow a square spot of ground. All savage nations possess, in the greatest perfection, the art of kindling or rather of making fire. The Indians carried with them for this purpose, the fibrous bark of the white cedar, previously rubbed to a powder between the hands, which being ignited in some mysterious manner, and blowed upon, a flame was produced. This they fed, first by the silky peelings of the birch bark and then by the bark itself, when the oily and bituminous matter burst forth into full action, and a splendid fire raised its flames and smoke amidst a huge pile of logs, to which each one contributed a share.

"The next thing was to rear some kind of a shelter; as we had neither wigwam or tent poles, we were obliged to find a substitute in the spruce boughs, which grew around in the greatest plenty; having erected these as a partial defence against the snow, which was still falling, we sat down determined to make the most of what was, under the circumstances, a source of real consolation—we enjoyed absolute rest—the snow scarcely touched our square, one side of which was bounded by a large tree, which lay stretched across it; against this our fire burned briskly—while on the opposite side, towards which I had turned my back, another very large tree was standing, and into the side of this latter, which was decayed and hollow, I had by degrees worked my way, and it formed an admirable shelter.

"And there we sat, listening to the crashes of the falling trees, and the cracking of their vast limbs, as they writhed and rocked in the tempest, creating the most awful and impressive sounds, while the snow banked up all around us like a white wall, resolutely maintained its position, not an atom yielding to the fierce crackling fire which blazed and sparkled so near it.

"After supper the Indians relapsed into their usual taciturnity,—one

"This was followed by a faint moan; one of the savages had sunk his tomahawk in her brain. She was then scalped, her body mutilated in a shocking manner, and thrown warm and bleeding into the flames." — *See Page 22.*

by one they lighted their tobacco pipes and continued smoking till a late hour, when dropping off by degrees, the whole party at last lay stretched out and snoring.

" This night, for the first time, they had neglected to bind us—perhaps they thought we would know better than to attempt an escape through the snow, so far from human habitations, where death from hunger and cold would be inevitable—and they judged rightly; our enormous fire had the effect of making me so comfortable, that only something of the most extraordinary nature, could have induced me to leave it. The scene was alike remarkable for its novelty and its dreariness; the volumes of smoke puffed and curled around me; the fire sparkled and snapped and threw out cinders, which burned holes in my clothes wherever they touched; large flakes of snow continued to fall, and heavy clots dropped occasionally upon the ground, and covered the sleeping figures of the men; the wind howled like an angry demon through the trees, whose majestic forms overshadowed us on every side, while the fire which rose so brilliantly and shed the light of day on the immediate surrounding objects, diffused a deeper gloom over the farther recesses of the forest. I had not the least inclination to sleep until near midnight. A solemn impression, tinged with melancholy, weighed heavily upon me; I thought of the fatigue I had undergone, and shuddered at the foreboding of what was to come. Distant scenes were brought to my recollection; my mother, dead and cold; my brothers, gone I knew not whither; myself a prisoner, a slave, condemned to a routine of ceaseless drudgery—then my eyes were lifted involuntarily towards heaven, and were finally attracted by the filmy wandering leaves of fire that ascended lightly over the tree tops, for a moment rivaling the stars in brightness, and then vanishing forever. ' Was ever a woman so singularly situated before?' I asked myself over and over again, as wrapping my buffalo skin around me, I sank down to enjoy for several hours, a refreshing and uninterrupted sleep.

" My master wakened me at daylight—I arose, feeling excessively cold, and found the whole party stirring The Indians were preparing breakfast, over a bed of living coals; the snow had ceased falling, the sky was clear, but the cold seemed more piercing and intense, if possible. My limbs were stiff and numb, while a soreness and aching in my ankles made me apprehend an attack of inflammation and swelling in the instep, which is often the painful consequence of wearing snow shoes, to those unaccustomed to their use. The morning, however, was bright and clear; the Indians anxious to proceed—we shared their breakfast with them, and such was the exhilarating effect of the keen, sharp air, that new strength and elasticity seemed diffused through all my frame.

" We had travelled, perhaps six miles, when the ice broke under one

2

of the Indians, and he was precipitated into the water; there was a piercing wind to increase the severity of the cold, and no house within reach—the other Indians hastened to the bank and kindled a fire with their best speed, but his feet were frosted before he could have the benefit of it; his companions held him at a moderate distance from the fire, and rubbed his limbs with snow till the circulation returned, and in little more than half an hour he was able to proceed.

"Notwithstanding the pain in my limbs, and the fatigue of drawing my sledge, I could not help remarking on the loveliness of nature peculiar to these northern latitudes, and which seemed sufficient to dissipate every sensation of pain and weariness; such a rare combination of frost and sunshine, without being seen and felt, could hardly be imagined. The wind, which had blown fiercely all the morning, came to a perfect lull in the afternoon; even the deep roar of the pine woods hushed to a gentle murmur—and as we walked along, our hair, our faces, our eye-brows, and even our eye-lashes, were as white as a powdering of snow could make them—while the warmth of the sun gave a sensation of peculiar purity to the air.

"Towards the end of this day's journey, the pain in my limbs and the lameness thereby occasioned, became a serious inconvenience. The inflammation in my feet and ankles was so acute as exactly to resemble the torture of the gout; to set my feet upon the ground was torture, and the slightest twist, when I trod in the holes made in the hard snow by the footsteps of those who went before, increased it—sometimes I was obliged to lie down in the snow, for relief, though the intense cold obliged me to rise almost immediately—I was sometimes tempted to crawl on my hands and knees, but even this motion gave me excessive torture. The poor boy, Frank Scott, was even worse off than myself, if possible, yet the Indians marched on with characteristic indifference, apparently altogether unconscious of our misery.

"Near sunset we reached the top of a hill, at the bottom of which lay the Indian village. The men with us, on seeing their native town, set up a wild and thrilling shout, which instantly communicated our approach to its inhabitants; they came thronging out in great numbers, looking so wild and fearful, that I was excessively frightened. I had heard dreadful stories about prisoners being compelled to run the gauntlet, and other terrible things. However, we were mercifully spared these trials; men, women and children seemed rather to regard us as objects of curiosity than malignancy and hatred; they ran around us, screeching and yelling, while the boldest came very near and examined our hands, our clothes, our hair, and our faces, with the utmost minuteness; the result was probably satisfactory, as some of them, after this, screamed and shouted with the most obstreperous laughter.

"I subsequently ascertained that my master belonged to the Missagua tribe of Indians, perhaps the least attractive of all these wild people, both with regard to their physical and mental endowments; the men are usually of small stature, with the coarsest and most repulsive features—the forehead is low and retreating; the ears large, and standing off from the face; the eyes looking towards the temples, keen, snake-like, and far apart; the cheek bones prominent; the nose long and flat, the nostrils very round; the jaw bone projecting, massy and brutal; the mouth expressing ferocity and sullen determination; the teeth large, even and dazzling white. There is a great difference however, in the countenances of the sexes. The lips of the female are fuller; the jaw less projecting, and the smile simple and agreeable. The women, too, are a merry, light-hearted set, and their constant laugh and incessant prattle form a strange contrast to the iron taciturnity of their grim lords. They surrounded me on all sides, and thus, amidst the noise of their chattering and laughing, the squalling of children and the barking of dogs, I was escorted into the village. This was simply a collection of huts, on the borders of a cedar swamp, and near the shores of a lake, called by the Indians, Umpha, though I am ignorant of the name it bears among the whites; a little farther off was a grove of maples, from which the Indian women made very good sugar. My master, who had recently lost his wife, took me to his wigwam, intending that I should fill her place. It will be readily concluded that I objected to this arrangement, though I willingly consented to prepare his food and keep his wigwam in order, which was no slight job; the Indian, however, was no very ardent wooer, he neither persecuted me with attentions himself or permitted others to do so; he seemed to think that time would reconcile me to their manner of living, in which event I would willingly become his wife. I found several white prisoners, all children, however, who hade been adopted into the tribe, and were fast losing, under surrounding influences, all traces of civilization. I was constantly visited by the females, who gave me lessons in all their various accomplishments of basket making, embroidering leggins and moccassins, carving bows, and forming a thousand little ornaments, in which an Indian especially delights. Certain it is, that I was not a very apt scholar; my thoughts were too busy about other things and scenes; I had not forgotten my home, though it was now a heap of ashes—not a day elapsed that I did not revolve in my mind some plan of escape, but I knew the success of my plan depended altogether on my manifesting an appearance of content. I could do nothing while jealously watched and guarded. I soon found that the chiefs and principal men of the tribe were absent on the war-path. I also found that southern emissaries had been among them, to stir them up into rebellion against the United

States; presents of blankets, rifles, ammunition and tobacco had been distributed amongst them by agents of Jefferson Davis, whom they had learned to style their Great Father. They had also experienced many heart-burnings about the payment of their annuities; then, too, the withdrawal of the troops usually stationed on the frontier, afforded them a fine opportunity for revolt. I believe that the first design of the Indians was to hold the prisoners as hostages, demanding a ransom in money or its equivalent, from their relatives or friends—not succeeding in this, their anger was aroused, hence the brutalities they practised upon their helpless victims.

As party after party came in with prisoners, I could not help noticing how differently they were treated. One man, whose name I never learned, but whom the Indians familiarly designated as 'Old Press,' and who was known to them as an active and dangerous enemy, was brought in one day, and they determined to avenge themselves upon him. He had been condemned to the fiery torture, and his body painted black, but by way of a previous amusement, he was manacled hand and foot, securely bound to an unbridled and unbroken horse, and driven off amid the shouts and whoops of the savages; the horse, frightenrd at his unwonted burden, reared and plunged, pitched and tore, and finding itself unable to shake him off, galloped with terrific speed towards the wood, jarring and bruising the rider at every step; at length, exhausted and subdued, it returned to the camp with its burden, amid the exulting shouts of the savages; they then removed the prisoner from the horse, and tied him to a stake, where, for twenty-four hours he remained in one position; he was then untied to run the gauntlet—several of the women insisted that I should go to witness the sport—the chief's wife, however, with more consideration than the rest, excused me, and rebuked the others.

"'Is not the white man her brother?' she asked, looking towards me, 'Can you think she desires to see him tortured? How would you like to see your brother's burned?'"

"This woman was a mountain of copper-colored flesh, but she had a remarkably good heart, which made her generally beloved, and gave her great influence over the others, though not sufficient to save the poor man. Three hundred Indians, men, women and children, armed with clubs and switches, arranged themselves in two parallel lines, to strike him as he passed; it was more than a mile to the council house, reaching which he was to be spared; he was started by a blow, on this encouraging race, but he soon broke through the files, and had almost reached the goal, when he was brought to the ground by a club—in this position he was beaten with the utmost severity, and again taken into custody. The Indians, however, instead of being satisfied with these terrible sufferings, were only stimulated to invent more ingenious tortures; still the fortitude of the victim was quite a match for their cruelty. He was compelled to run the gauntlet again and again; he was exposed to insult of every kind, and subjected to all manner of privations and injuries; sometimes he was bound in the most uncomfortable positions; at others he was beaten, pinched, dragged on the ground, and deprived for long periods, of sleep. Many of the females seemed to take delight in rehearsing the story of his sufferings in my hearing—how he would be dragged from village to village, that all might witness, be entertained, and assist in his tortures—but they also bore testimony to the courage and endurance with which he sustained his sufferings, and expressed a conviction that so brave and valiant a man would ultimately escape.

"At last a chief, named the 'Buffalo,' who had been out on a hunting expedition, returned with his party. He was immediately informed that a white prisoner was soon to be led to the stake—he went to see him, and instantly recognized an old friend, with whom he had hunted near the head waters of the Great Missouri, and who had once saved his life from the the spring of a Catamount. The savage made himself known, raised up his old friend, and promised to exert his influence in his behalf: he summoned a council at once, descanted on the courage and fortitude of the prisoner, (qualities which the Indians admire even in an enemy,) and persuaded them to resign their captive to him, after a while they consented; he took the unfortunate man to his wigwam—fed, nursed and cared for him until he completely recovered, when he accompanied him to within a few miles of the white settlements.

" Sometime during the month of February, the Indians brought in a young man, a captive, whom I recognized at once as an old friend and neighbor—and the recognition was mutual—for though both were prisoners, neither was deprived of the use of his or her eyes; then, too, I was much less jealously guarded than at first, and when my master was absent, which was often, we found abundant opportunities for interviews and conversation. Instead of becoming reconciled to the Indian mode of life, I experienced each day a feeling of deeper disgust with all that I saw. The men were brutal, while the most deplorable want of chastity characterised the women. Even the little children were deficient in the usual grace and sweetness of childhood; their amusements all partook of their savage nature, while to moral or intellectual enjoyments they were entire strangers. Their sense of hearing, sight and smell, are much more acute than those of white people, and enables them to distinguish objects at an incredible distance; they would see to distinguish birds in·the air so high up that I could not discover the smallest speck; they sometimes heard wild animals crackling and breaking the bushes, and going out with their bows or rifles, would kill and bring them in, when I failed to hear the faintest sound, though intently listen-ing; many of them would follow a trail by its scent, the same as a hound, and they would easily tell the sex of the wearer by the scent of a garment.

"The Indians are particularly susceptible to little acts of kindness and affection; I soon discovered this, and strove by every means in my power to secure their good will; I have every reason to believe that I succeeded to a great degree. I wished to attach some of them to my person, and engage their friendship and assistance against the time that I should make an attempt to escape.

"There was one young girl of fifteen, a half breed, and truly beautiful, whose history was quite as interesting as her appearance. She was the offspring of misfortune—her father had been drowned by breaking through the ice on one of the Upper Lakes, while out fishing; her mother, a Canadian woman, and quite as bold and courageous as a man, went to his assistance, but not in time to save him, though she succeeded in recovering his body; being near her confinement with this child, the fright and grief brought on premature labor, and she died, leaving her infant to the care of her husband's sister.

The superstitious Indians consider the soul of one that is drowned to be accursed, and according to their belief, he is not permitted to enter the happy hunting-grounds of the immortals. His spirit, on the con-trary, is supposed to haunt the lake or river in which he lost his life; his body is buried on some lonely island, which the Indians never pass without leaving a small portion of food, ammunition, or tobacco, to supply his wants; his children are considered unlucky, and few willingly unite themselves to the females of the family, lest a portion of the father's curse should light on them.

"This poor orphan girl generally kept aloof from the rest, never joining the amusements of others of her age, and seeming altogether so lonely and companionless, that my heart was insensibly attracted towards her, and a feeling of hearty sympathy and good will sprang up between us. Her features were small and regular; her face oval, and her large, dark, loving eyes, were full of tenderness and sensibility, but bright and shy as those of the deer; her complexion was a clear olive, suffused on her cheeks and lips with the richest vermillion, while her even and pearly teeth were of dazzling whiteness; her stature was small; her limbs plump and beautifully rounded; her hands and feet delicate, and her figure elastic and graceful. She was altogether a beautiful child of nature, and her name, in the Indian language, signified the frozen water. We often exchanged visits, and finally she came to reside altogether in the cabin of my master. I entrusted her with the secret of my design to escape, and though she wept bitterly at the idea of parting, she said nothing to dissuade me. Indeed, she promised to render us all the assistance in her power—for it had been already settled that the young man alluded to before, whose name was Hiram Johnson, should accompany me.

"He was a brave, stout, young fellow, thoroughly acquainted with the Indian character, and accustomed to prairie life, and hunting adventures; he had spent some time in the Upper Missouri country, among the Blackfeet and Cassinaboin tribes; he found that in spite of the numerous treaties between them and the Federal Government, a hostile feeling generally prevailed, by which the danger of travelling through that region was greatly augmented; hence, he proposed that we should strike off in a southeasterly direction, in order to reach, if possible, the white settlements on the Minnesota river.

"It was yet in early spring, when the whole Indian village was thrown into the greatest consternation. A runner from the Sioux nation had arrived with information that a detachment of United States troops were on their way to attack and punish all the tribes who had been concerned in the recent outbreak, with the demand that all the prisoners should be at once restored, that too, without ransom.

"It would not, perhaps, be proper to say that the Indians are naturally cowards, but they do fear, more than any other people, a hostile demonstration of regular troops. An immediate council was called; men, women and children ran from place to place, whooping and screaming. Some proposed to kill the prisoners, and then deny all participation in the outrages; others declared, that however feasible this plan might appear, it would not do. It was finally suggested that the whole village should literally pull up stakes and move still farther off. With inexpressible pain I heard the nature of their decision, and at once resolved to escape, if possible. As to accompanying them in their journey, I felt that death would be preferable. I knew instinctively, that there would be great difficulty in pushing forward through a wild and unexplored country, intersected with rivers, lakes and woods—at the outset covered with snow, and on the approach of warmer weather, so flooded and marshy as to render travelling on foot excessively fatiguing. Nor was this all; the voracity, improvidence and indolence of the men, subjected the females to repeated distress. If from fishing or hunting, a larger supply than usual was procured, instead of using it with moderation, and laying up a store for future necessities, all was devoured at once; when the savages, gorged like the boa, coiled themselves up and remained in a state of stupidity until again roused to activity by the calls of hunger.

"For my own part, I had constantly suffered for the want of wholesome provision, as the men always appropriated all the best of the fare, leaving the bones and refuse for the women. Some times, too, we found it almost impossible to build a fire, in consequence of the moisture from the melting snow, which saturated the brushwood. Usually it was all feasting or all famine; we were often one, two and even three days without food—on these occasions the Indians would examine their wardrobes with the utmost care, in order to decide what part they could best spare, when perhaps, a half rotten deer skin, or a pair of old moccassins would be sacrificed to relieve their extreme hunger. As I could not and would not partake of such delectable dishes, my sufferings admitted less alleviations than did theirs. It is scarcely possible for one to imagine the pangs of hunger, who has not experienced them; and in wandering situations like that now proposed, the hardships is greatly aggravated by the uncertainty with regard to its duration, and the means most proper to be used to remove it, as well as by the labor and fatigue we must necessarily undergo for that purpose, and the dissappointments which too often frustrate our best concerted plans and most strenuous exertions. I found, by sad experience, that hunger not only enfeebles the body, but depresses the spirits, in spite of every effort to prevent it. Many a time did my stomach so far lose its digestive powers as only to resume its office with pain and weariness; more than once was I reduced to so low a state by hunger, that when Providence threw any thing in my way, my stomach was only able to retain the smallest portion, without producing the most excessive pain.

"The houses of the Indians, as well as their canoes, being made of skin, and exceedingly light and portable, the removal of a whole village was not an undertaking of any great magnitude. These habitations were so near alike, that a description of one would serve for the whole; that of my master was oval, about fifteen feet long, ten feet wide in the middle, and eight feet at either end. It was dug a few inches below the surface, one half being covered with skins which served as a seat and bed for the family. In the middle of the other half a space about four feet wide, had been hollowed out and was the only place where a full grown man could stand erect. One side of this formed the hearth. The door in one end of the house, was about three feet high by two wide, and consisted simply of a curtain of skins. On the top was an orifice of about eighteen inches square, which served the triple purpose of a window, a chimney, and an occasional door. The covering was of skins stretched on tent poles, the lower ends of which were fastened in the ground, while the upper was lashed to a stick bent so as to form a bow.

" When preparing for removal, these coverings are taken off, the poles loosened from the earth, and all firmly lashed together. Sometimes sledges are provided on which the whole is mounted, together with pots, kettles, pans, canoes, and such provisions, ammunition and tobacco, as they happen to have on hand. At other times all this luggage is carried upon the backs of the women, the girls and the dogs; among whom it is very equally apportioned, according to the strength of the bearer.

"Being well aware that I should have to carry my master's tent, all the furniture and cooking utensils that it contained, or drag the sledge on which they were placed, I determined to elope that very night, though I was really half starved and nearly naked. I had not learned to prepare the deer skin clothing used by the Indians at this season, and even if I had it is very doubtful whether my master would have furnished me with the skins; as he had taken great umbrage because I steadfastly refused to become his wife,—I sometimes thought that he delighted in subjecting me to hardships and indignities. The only clothing he ever allowed me was his own worn out and cast off apparel, with an old blanket which had served his favorite dog for a bed, until it sickened and died.

"During my sojourn among the Indians, I had accidentally discovered a small opening in the side of a hill, which ran along the borders of the lake, at the distance of a mile from the village. This opening I had once entered, crawling on my hands and knees, until it expanded into an apartment of considerable extent. I felt certain that the Indians were ignorant of its existence, as I had never heard it alluded to by them, hence, I conceived the idea of hiding there a few days, until the ardour of pursuit should be past. Johnson, however, opposed this measure, 'We should certainly be discovered,' he said, 'and retaken in which event our sufferings would be greatly augmented.'

"I did not readily understand how this could be, so far as I was concerned, and I told him so; told him likewise, that he could do as he liked, but my resolution was taken that I would escape that night. Luckily my master brought in a deer during the afternoon, and as I was called upon to dress it, I tood good care to appropriate a large po⋅ \on to myself; I also took spears, arrow-heads, fish-hooks, a knife, a t⋅mahawk, an apparatus for striking fire, and sundry other articles, that I conjectured would be useful on my long and adventurous journey.

"Early in the afternoon, the south-wind began to blow, which the Indians declared was the fore-runner of a thaw; and a thaw just then they dreaded, as it would seriously interfere with their plans of removing. Simultaneous with this, another runner from the Sioux, brought intelligence that several of the Chiefs and head men, who had been prominent actors in the massacre of the whites, had been taken prisoners, tried by court-martial and civil processes, and condemned to be hung. He also asserted, that the United States authorities were making every exertion to find out and arrest such others, as had been guilty of the same crime. This news gave them all a new start, and though it began to rain tremendously, and every thing was just as wet as it could be, the preparations went on with alacrity. They had taken the precaution of sending a small party in advance, to open the way, and to ascertain that there was no danger or impediment in the route they had chosen. They certainly feared the white man; all their talk was of white men their power and their cruelties;

"Some one in my hearing proposed sending a deputation to the whites, entreating their forbearance and asking peace. For a few minutes after this, intense silence prevailed, when an old Chief perhaps eighty years of age, uttered his dissent in something like the following words.

"I am for war, war to the knife! My rifle is true to its aim, my tomahawk is sharp! I have taken many scalps in my younger days, I can still take more. White men are great liars! White men kill Indian just as they kill deer? White men see squaw, they shoot her right down; shoot papoose the same as rabbit! I no like White men, white men no like me!"

"When he had finished, another chief related his grievances as follows:

"'I once had a son,' he said, 'a son who was a brave chief, and so kind to his old father and mother, that he hunted game for them to eat; one day he was out hunting deer, and the rifle of the white man killed him—the sun set; the night came, still he had not returned; his mother, unable to sleep, went to look for her son—she followed his trail a long way through the thick bushes—at the dawn of day the mother and son were both gone, and the old chief was very lonely; he went out to look for his wife and child—he found them both, but both were dead; the white man's bullet had pierced their bosoms; the white man's knife had tore the scalp from their heads! Ask me not to make peace with the white man!'

"I felt my cheeks burn, and the blood tingle in my veins. I knew these accusations were in a great part true; I knew that many wanton and unprovoked outrages had been inflicted upon them. No one could have blamed them for repelling their assailants; but the wholesale massacre of innocent and defenceless families, was quite another thing, so was their practice of condemning poor little captive children to starvation; many a time have I seen these innocents, who had been carried off from their parents, almost in a state of nudity, digging in the snow with their fingers, for grass-nuts, or any roots, to afford sustenance. No more piteous sight was ever beheld than those naked infants in bitter old weather; on the open snow, reduced by starvation to living skeletons, with the certainty that in the event of their death, they would be thrown out in the wilderness for the wolves to devour.

"Those who prate of the beauties of a state of nature, should live among the Indians and see savage life as I have seen it, I think they would become quite as disgusted with it as I did.

"It was sometime past midnight when the cavalcade took up its line of march. The night was intensely dark, and a steady rain falling, prevented the use of torches. It was utterly impossible to see the least thing; but the concert of strange sounds, gabbling, whooping, yelling, children squalling, and dogs barking, was perfectly deafening. Wrapped in their blankets and furs, and maintaining the utmost gravity and sedateness, the men went first—the women and children, with the baggage, bringing up the rear; my friend, the orphan girl, had volunteered to drag my sledge, and I knew that in the darkness it was impossible that I should be missed, still it was not without misgivings that I fell behind and suffered the company to go on, leaving me alone in the woods. In my anxiety to escape, I had scarcely calculated on the thousand dangers with which I should be environed when once left to my own resources; now a conviction of the whole almost overpowered me—it was but a moment, however; I felt that I was in the hands of an Almighty Protector, who cared, 'even for the fall of a sparrow,' I would confide myself to him, not doubting that he would eventually guide me in safety to my friends.

"Of my fellow prisoner, Johnson, I knew nothing. Two days had elapsed since I had seen him. I should not be missed before the morning, possibly not then, still I felt assured that when he once discovered my absence, he would seek me at the cave. In the cave, therefore, I determined to remain for a few days. But the first difficulty was to get there, and in the darkness I was not sure of my course.

"The first thing upon attempting to move, I stumbled over a large basswood log, I recollected seeing this before, and knew that it was hollow; here, then, I might obtain shelter from the storm, at least for that night. I crept within it, and notwithstanding my agitation and anxiety, soon fell asleep. When I awoke next morning, the sun was shining, and the weather having greatly moderated during the night, was really pleasant. I felt the necessity of the greatest caution, as there are always more or less stragglers left behind, who stay to gather up such fragments as have been either lost or accidently mislaid. On this occasion, however, the fear of the white men seems to have prevented all wish or desire in any one to remain behind. Before peering out, I listened intently; not a sound was to be heard but the voices of nature—the deep, hollow murmuring of the woods—the distant roar of the water-fall and the chirping of some early spring birds. Encouraged by the silence, I ventured to leave the place of my concealment, and proceeded with trembling steps towards the cave, anxiously looking around, and often starting, as the breeze rustled amongst the trees, mistaking it for the whisperings of men.

"The snow had all departed, and many little streams which emptied into the lake, were running briskly. Knowing the Indian skill in following a trail, I immediately entered the water, and walked in it a considerable distance; at length emerging near the entrance of the cave, and taking another survey of the woods, to make sure that I was not watched, I cautiously secreted myself therein; all was perfectly dark, and the chilly air made me shake as with the ague. I had all the materials for kindling a fire, but feared to use them, lest the smoke might attract my enemies. I felt around and found a small cache of provisions, which I had almost starved myself to save, in anticipation of this period. I ate but sparingly, wishing to reserve as much as possible for future use. I remained in the cavern that day and night, without seeing any one, and, Oh! how tedious the time appeared. I could not sleep all the time; I feared to move in the darkness, lest I might get bewildered and lost; I had no resources of reading or conversation, and my thoughts were not the most agreeable; however, I was on my way to home and freedom. I could not remain patiently where I was and determined if nothing happened to prevent, to resume my journey next morning, with, or without the company of Johnson.

"When morning came my resolution was unshaken, and the cheerful beams of the sun, playing on my sight, re-animated my spirits; I gathered all my provisions, and whatever I designed to take with me in a small bundle, and came out into the open air; here I stood for a few minutes, listening, but no sound met my ear, save the sighing of the wind among the trees. I passed around to the borders of the lake without seeing any person, and everything looked exactly as I had last seen it; it was evident no one had been there, then I paused, and looking at the sun made a mental calculation of the route I should take to reach the nearest white settlement. Again, I looked around to make certain that no one was following, and this time saw—heaven help me—an Indian whom I instantly recognised to be my master; I neither screamed nor fainted, but stood like one petrified with horror and amazement. His back was towards me, and from his manner and attitude I felt certain that he had not discovered my presence, but how long could this continue; the least noise on my part would certainly attract his attention, even were it no more than the rustling of leaves or the breaking of a twig. To remain where I was, would be attended with almost certain discovery; to attempt concealment, was almost equally so; what then could I do?

"While standing thus irresolute, the crack of a rifle resounded through the forest, and the Indian fell; a ball having penetrated his brain. Without waiting to ascertain whether a friend or foe was near, I turned and fled; fear lending wings to my steps, neither did I venture to look back, though a voice called upon me to stop, and I heard steps advancing in quick pursuit. Before I could reach the cavern my breath failed, and I leaned against a tree for support; the man came up and gazed upon me with a strong expression of curiosity and surprise. He assumed a gentle manner, assured me I had nothing to fear from him, and inquired if I had escaped from the Indians; I was really too terrified and out of breath to speak, when he continued his questions and assurances.

"'You have nothing to fear from me,' he said, 'and if I can render you any assistance, I shall be only too happy to do so, was this devil back here looking for you?' he continued, 'let me lift his hair, and then we'll be jogging; that is, if you do not object to my company.'

" Turning back to where the Indian was laying dead, he tore off his reeking scalp before I had time to remonstrate, cut and bent a bow, and placed the skin upon it in exact Indian fashion. I closed my eyes with a sickening sensation of horror.

"'It's just what he would have done by me, had the opportunity offered' he remarked, by way of apology, 'but I think the sooner we leave this place the better for both of us; this way madam,' and he struck off through the woods.

" We travelled for some time in perfect silence, and I had ample opportunity to mark the features and manners of my preserver. He was dressed in hunting costume which well became his athletic form, he had a roman nose, with a fine intelligent countenance, and his thick black hair was brushed off his high and expansive forehead. At last he stopped suddenly and turning his face full upon mine, asked.

"'Where do you wish to go, young woman?'

"'Almost anywhere among white people,' I answered; 'my mother, my sister, and my brothers were slain; I am without relatives altogether, but I trust that the story of my misfortunes will find me friends.'

"'It certainly ought to,' replied the man, 'but now you stay right here,' he continued, 'behind the shadow of this rock while I go back.'

"'What for?' I asked involuntarily.

"'To strip that red-skin.'

"'And bury him.'

"'No indeed; tne wolves may pick his bones for all I care, but he has a rifle and a tomahawk, the very things for you to have.'

" I thanked him for the interest he took in my welfare, concealed myself behind the rock, and waited patiently for his return. In a remarkably short time he came, bringing the weapons and ammunition of the fallen warrior   These he gave to me, bidding me keep a good heart, and use them, if necessary, for my safety.

"That night he told me his story.   It was almost identical with that of hundreds of others.   He had been one of an exploring party, and went out to shoot deer; some of the Sioux Indians were shooting ducks, and hearing the explosion of fire-arms, they marked the direction and followed the white men to their camp.   They were most inveterate beggars, and stole whatever they could lay their hands on.   The white men ordered them out, and force was used to take away their fire-arms. In the scuffle one of the Americans was severely wounded with a knife, and some of the Indians were killed; the survivors sought their camp, made a fictitious scalp of horse-hair, which they erected on a pole, and commenced the war-dance.   The other Indians joined, until finally, wrought up to a pitch of the greatest fury, they sallied out, sought the white men's camp, which they attacked while the party were breakfasting, under cover of the willows, which grew on the banks of the creek. Captain Engleson the leader, was the first man who had finished his breakfast; he arose, and while speaking to his men, the Indians with a tremendous yell fired upon them.   Captain Engleson raised his hands and beckoned them to stop; the men immediately fled, only one man fell by the first fire of the Indians; the men's first endeavors were to reach their horses, the Indians pursued and shot them; the whole party with the exception of this one man was exterminated; he was severely wounded, and crawled off into a hollow, where the Indians found him two or three days after the massacre.

"A large body of Emigrants was encamped a short distance off.   They heard the firing, and a company of horsemen galloped to the scene of action, in the fierce expectation of offensive warfare.

"They arrived on the spot; they saw the mutilated remains of the white men, but no signs of Indians.   The weather was very cold, the ground frozen hard; they had nothing with them but their swords to dig into the frozen earth, and were thus compelled to leave the dead unburied. Months after this their bones were seen bleaching on the prairie, a hideous monument of Indian attrocity.

"My companion whose name was Webb, related all this, though not in the exact language which I have used.

"'But how did you manage to escape?' I asked when he had concluded.

"'I watched for an opportunity the same as yourself,' he answered, 'though it was some time before one offered, I was so jealously guarded. At last their vigilance somewhat relaxed.   I was sent out to hunt accompanied by two Indians; one of these I shot when his back was towards me; the other I assailed and knocked down with the butt end of my rifle.   You will readily believe, that I didn't leave him while

"While standing thus irresolute, the crack of a rifle resounded through the forest, and the Indian fell, a ball having penetrated his brain."—*See Page* 44

breath was in his body, and that the grass didn't grow under my feet
when I had got his scalp.'

"'How long ago was this?' I asked.

"'Six weeks to-morrow.'

"'And since that time you have been like myself a wanderer in the
woods.'

"'Something of the kind, I must confess' he replied.

"'Have you been without fire all this time?' I inquired, for it seemed
to me then, that warmth was the greatest blessing on earth.

"'Not quite,' he answered.

"'And think you we can have a fire to-morrow night?' I asked, with
something of anxiety as to the answer.

"'That depends altogether upon our situation, and whether there are
Indians in the neighborhood.'

"'Are there Indians near us now?'

"'Not very far off I discovered signs of them this afternoon.'

"'And didn't tell me.'

"'I feared you would be alarmed.'

"'And so I should. The very thought of being made their prisoner
again, thrills me with horror.'

"'You never shall be while I live,' he answered.

"And thus we talked nearly the whole night, as the cold prevented
our sleeping, and we feared to make a fire lest the smoke should betray
our hiding-place.

"In this climate a thaw usually lasts a few days, when the cold re-
turns with redoubled vigor. The next morning we found this exem-
plified. The snow commenced falling, and the wind blew a perfect
hurricane. In consequence of the fleecy drift we conld only see a few
feet ahead, while the violence of the wind almost carried us off our legs.
The snow soon increased to such a depth that walking became both
difficult and painful. Webb proposed to encamp under the shelter of a
little wood; I could offer no objections, and while we were making
preparations, an Indian woman suddenly appeared. We both stood on
the defensive, but she gave us to understand by signs, that she was
quite alone and friendly. Webb who partly understood her language,
assured me that I had nothing to fear, and when she tendered us her
hospitality he cheerfully accepted it. We followed her to a wild part of
the country, remote from any human habitation, where was a small hut
in which she had lived for many months entirely alone. She recounted
with affecting simplicity the circumstances, which had induced her to
dwell in solitude. She belonged she said, to the Mohahoe Indians, and
during an inroad of the Sioux, in 1861, had been taken prisoner; the
savages, according to their usual custom, stole upon the tents in the

3

night, and murdered before her face, her entire family, father, mother brothers, sisters and husband, while she and another young woman were reserved from the slaughter and made prisoners. Her child, an infant a few months old, she managed to conceal in some clothing, but on arriving at the place where the women was, it was discovered and immediately killed.

" This horrid cruelty had nearly upset her reason, and she made a solemn vow to escape the first opportunity, and return to her own nation; but the great distance and the innumerable creeks and rivers she had to pass, caused her to loose the way, and winter coming on she built a hut, and lived happy and contented. At this time she was the finest Indian woman I had ever seen, in good health and well fed. Her cabin was very comfortable, and she had snow shoes and other useful articles, all the produce of her own industry. For subsistence she snared partridges, squirrels and rabbits, and had killed two or three deer and some beaver. From the sinews of their legs, she twisted thread with great dexterity, which she employed in sewing her clothing, and making snares. This clothing was formed of rabbit's skins sewed together; the materials, though rude, being tastefully disposed, so as to make her garb assume a pleasing though desert-bred appearance.

" No sooner had we reached her habitation, than she set about preparing us something to eat, and though her cookery was of the rudest kind, the food was nourishing and palatable. So well were we both pleased with our amiable hostess, that Webb proposed remaining till the spring broke. Providence however had determined otherwise.

" On the third day after our arrival, she went out as usual to attend to her snares, but returned almost immediately, her limbs trembling, and her countenance blanched with consternation. A party of her old enemies, the Sioux, were encamped less than half a mile off. She did not think they had discovered her as yet, though how soon they might she could not tell. She evidently considered it unsafe to remain in that neighborhood and proposed an immediate departure; I invited her to go with us. Webb insisted and she finally consented; I really considered her a great acquisition, and felt much safer in her company. She had a small sledge of her own construction, on which her property side by side with mine was placed. Being light it scarcely impeded her progress in the least and she went ahead, wearing her snow-shoes with the ease and agility of a man. Although she said not a word I could readily divine her purpose; she thought our safety lay not so much in precipitate flight, as in reaching some stream or river, down which we could pass in a boat, thus leaving no trail behind us. Even Webb could not keep up with her, I did not begin to try. When by looking back she could see us no longer, she would set down at the foet of a tree, and wait till we came up.

"Thus we journeyed two days, resting at night in a shelter which the red woman formed by placing her sledge in an upright position, supported by strips of bark. On the third day, towards evening, we found ourselves in a wild valley, which neither of my companions had ever seen before. The red woman, ahead, as usual, paused suddenly, her countenance expressive of alarm—Webb soon approached her, when she informed him that she heard sticks cracking behind us, and was confident that Indians were near; Webb, being an experienced hunter, and from habit grown indifferent to the dangers of the woods, diverted himself pretty freely at her expense; the woman, whose Indian name was Sunny Eye, was not so easily satisfied—she declared that in whatever direction she turned, the same ominous sounds continued to haunt her, and as Webb treated her fears with the most perfect indifference, she determined to act upon her own responsibility; gradually slackening her pace, until I came up, she motioned me to conceal myself in a dense thicket of dwarf cedars, that grew near by, and immediately afterwards she suddenly sprung aside and disappeared between the banks of a deep ravine.

"Scarcely was this accomplished, when to my unspeakable terror I beheld two savages put aside the branches of some whortleberry bushes and look out cautiously in the direction Webb had taken. Though I never had skill in fire-arms, I raised my rifle, and it exploded. The act was one of madness, and I quickly repented my temerity; both savages sprang towards me with uplifted tomahawks—the motion was seen by the Sunny Eye, who raised her rifle and fired, while I ran away through the bushes—one of the Indians fell severely wounded, and the other one started after her; Webb, however, who had heard the firing, was coming back, and seeing the Indian, sent a bullet through his breast. Thus, we were fortunately preserved from this danger, still we could not feel safe. In every shadow we feared a foeman; behind every bush we anticipated a lurking enemy; the most ordinary sounds, the cry of a panther, the howl of a wolf, or the hooting of an owl, seemed ominous of danger; still we pressed on bravely, always hoping for the best.

"The next day we came to a region that bore in all its parts, the marks of Indian outrages. Cabins deserted and burned; plantations laid waste; the mouldering remains of cattle and horses; hogs and poultry running wild; the fair country once teeming with life and industry, now entirely desolate. At one place, near the banks of a small river, a battle had been fought, and the snow, beat and trampled by the wolves, did not altogether hide the mangled and mutilated remains of the dead. While yet lingering here, we observed a thicket of low bushes to shake violently, and the next moment the face of a white man peered anxiously out.

" Webb advanced towards him, when he crawled still nearer, drawing his limbs painfully after him, and it soon became apparent that he had been most fearfully wounded in the engagement that had recently taken place.

" It seemed that the inhabitants, hearing of the hostile approach of the Indians, had met and determined on self defence ; they were badly defeated, however, not from want of bravery, but the ovewhelming superiority of numbers. The white men were but a small party of undisciplined farmers, and half grown boys ; the Indians numbered a large party of experienced warriors. The result might have been foreseen ; it was in every respect disastrous. The whites gave way ; they were pursued by the savages with the utmost eagerness. The river was filled with cakes and lumps of floating ice, and very difficult to cross ; many were killed in the attempt and many more were taken prisoners ; a fate worse than death. Some escaped on horseback, others on foot and in a few hours the melancholy news filled the whole country with consternation. Meanwhile, the Indians were spreading destruction on all sides ; mangling and mutilating the slain, and torturing the living.

" ' And how did you escape ?' inquired Webb, when the wounded man had finished his story.

" ' That I can hardly tell, myself,' he answered, 'though in the uproar and confusion incident to the fight I managed to get away somehow, but you had better not stay here any longer than is absolutely necessary,' he said, glancing curiously around, 'it is impossible to tell what eyes may be looking for us now.'

" ' And what will become of you,' asked Webb, gazing upon the battered frame of the pioneer; it is very evident that you cannot walk.'

" ' Walk no; I shall never walk again ; I expect to stay where I am, and die of my wounds when the time comes; well, I don't care; we must all die sometime, and a few years sooner or later can make little difference; I have neither wife nor child; the Indians killed them; I am alone in the world.'

" ' I don't see how you have managed to subsist,' said Webb.

" ' Easily enough,' returned the other ' I am not particular and dead animals are laying all around ; don't you see?'

" ' Webb did see, and not being very fastidious himself, the idea of sharing a meal with the dogs and vultures, did not strike him as particularly horrible or unpleasant.

" ' But we cannot leave you here to die all alone,' I said; 'it would be little better than murder.'

" ' White man go,' said Sunny Eye, pointing to her sledge.

"'Yes, you must mount that sledge and go with us,' I exclaimed, 'no hesitation, no refusal, we will not hear it.'

"'To be dragged by women,' ejaculated the Pioneer, 'never.'

"'Rather than you should perish here, I will drag you myself,' said Webb.

"'Oh, very well, then; but women are women, and I could never think of taxing their strength.'

"It required our united exertions to get him upon the sledge. His wounds, when examined, seemed to be doing well, though had he been less hardy, less sound in health and constitution, and also less comfortably protected by fur clothing, he would certainly have perished before our finding him.

"Sunny Eye, however, persisted in dragging the sledge.

"'Man can't, don't know how,' she said.

"It was decided to let her have her own way.

"It was decided, too, that it would be much better, perhaps safer, to float down the river, but we had no boat, and though the Sunny Eye possessed the materials, and could very well have constructed one of sufficient size and strength to have merely crossed a stream, but one to bear a long voyage, and laden, too, was quite another thing.

"So far, we had fared pretty well for food, and my strength had held out a great deal better than I expected that it would. Game had been tolerable plenty, and we had managed to kill enough to make us comfortable, could we have seasoned and prepared it rightly. Still, I felt my strength gradually departing; the cold and the exposure—the constant fatigue and weariness, was telling badly upon my frame. One of my feet was frozen, and I walked with pain and great difficulty. On this occasion my lameness had so increased, that I was always far behind, and my energy and firmness almost deserted me. Night approached, and we looked in vain for a place of shelter—naught but a desert waste of eternal snow met our anxious gaze. Faint, and almost exhausted, I sat down on the snow bank, my feet resting in the tracks of those who had gone before; I was seriously revolving in my mind whether I would go farther, or set still and die where I was: even then I felt a sleepiness stealing over me, and knew that sleep would end in that eternal repose which wakes only in another world.

"Suddenly I heard my name called; this aroused me, and once fairly aroused, I felt the wickedness and folly of the act I had been meditating. My life was not my own, to throw away; I was in the hands of God, who in his own good time would take me to himself, or restore me to my friends. I arose hastily, breathing a mental prayer; Webb was coming back on the trail, and it was his voice I had heard.

"It was now dusk, the cold had much increased, and a fearful snow storm was setting in.

"Again he called my name; it appeared he had not yet discovered me, and this time I answered.

"'Oh, there you are!' he exclaimed, 'We feared you had wandered off and got lost somewhere. Please walk a little faster, can you? I have good news."

"'Ah! what is it?'

"'We have found a good, comfortable house down yonder, all ready furnished, with beds, provisions and every thing necessary.'

"'Why, how strange!'

"'The inhabitants must have fled in their fear of the Indians; fled too precipitately to remove their goods.'

"'And the Indians never went there?'

"'Not at all. But such things often happen; I remember once when the news came of an Indian outbreak, in the Black Hawk War, the frontier inhabitants hurried off in such speed, that some left candles burning on their tables; supper half eaten, upon the plates, and the bread half baked, in the oven.'

"'It is not to be wondered at—there is nothing so terrible as these Indian massacres,' I answered.

"It was now quite dark, though I could just discern a light faintly glimmering through a pine grove, at a little distance ahead.

"Webb saw it, too.

"'How careless!' he exclaimed, 'They should have darkened the window and stopped all the holes, before kindling a fire. That would serve as a beacon light to guide the Indians to us, for miles.'

"We hurried along as fast as I was able to go for my lameness. At length Webb spoke.

"'I hope you had no notion of giving out?'

"I did not answer him directly, but only inquired what made him think that I had.

"'Oh, I can guess pretty well when one is low-spirited and desponding.'

"'Well, you cannot wonder that I am so?'

"'Oh no; you, as well as the rest of us, have been exposed to uncommon hardships: and he went on to descant on the prospect of our soon arriving at some settlement, and the necessity there was for mutual encouragement, instead of vain regrets and despondency; the difficulties were to be met, and it depended on ourselves whether we should return to our friends or perish in the wilderness.'

"He said that nothing in all his life had so fully confirmed his belief

"The next instant a dreadful apprehension seized me—a mingled cry of joy and sorrow, of pleasure and apprehension, broke from my lips "—*See Page* 65.

m an overruling Providence, as our coming so opportunely upon that house, filled as it was with every needful comfort.

"I felt the force of his remarks, and determined for the future, to place my trust more entirely in heaven.

"We reached the house and entered. Sunny Eye had already built a good fire, from the wood which lay in one corner of the fire-place. Oh, how comfortable it seemed; how unlike anything I had realized since my captivity; still, so great was the pain of my frozen limbs on coming near the fire, that I immediately retired to bed, thinking it would be impossible for me to proceed the next day; nor was any refreshment from sleep to be expected. Sunny Eye prepared supper, but I could not eat; the pain actually made me sick at my stomach. The moment her culinary operations were over, Sunny Eye left the house without saying a word—she was gone so long, we began to fear some misfortune had happened to her; we could hear the distant howling of wolves, and at this season of the year they are particularly ferocious. Could it be possible she had fallen a victim to their hunger?

"'No, no!' said Webb, 'Not the least danger of that, she'll take care of herself, never you fear.'

"'But where can she have gone?'

"'It is impossible to say.'

"'I hope she has not deserted us.'

"'So do I, yet I have heard of such things.'

"'She cannot have become offended?'

"'We have given her no cause, at any rate.'

"The door opened very quietly, and the Indian woman came in just as she had gone out, so still, silent and reserved, that no one appeared to notice her.

"Yet I did notice her, and I saw at once that she carried an armful of roots and simples, from which she instantly set about preparing a decoction.

"I guessed her purpose.

"'Is that for me?' I asked.

"She made a gesture of assent; for though she could understand my language tolerably well, hers was the same as Greek to me.

"Webb and his companion sat smoking in silence, and finally dropped off to sleep; while she busied herself in preparing the remedy. How she did it, or what were the ingredients, I do not know. When it was ready, she spread it on a piece of untanned deer skin, and bound it closely around my aching limbs: it acted like a charm—I experienced instantaneous relief, and fell at once into a pleasant slumber.

"How long this lasted, I cannot tell, but I was awakened suddenly, by the discharge of a rifle, which produced a most tremendous explosion;

the sound reverberated along the rocks and was re-echoed by the valley. Instantly we were all up, and the word, 'Indians,' was on every tongue. Listening intently, we soon became conscious of other sounds—the distant gallop of a horse, and the most terrific howling of wolves, that seemed to approach nearer and nearer.

" ' What could it mean ? ' I looked at Webb for a solution.

" ' Some benighted traveler is being pursued by the wolves ! ' he exclaimed, 'They are ravenous with hunger.'

" ' Oh, heaven ! '

" ' It is even so."

" ' What can we do to assist him ? '

" ' That would be hard to tell.'

" Nearer and nearer came the sounds. The wolves howling and yelping in full chorus.

" ' Oh ! something must be done,' I cried, really alarmed at the impending fate of the traveler.'

" Webb took his rifle and sallied out ; Sunny Eye uttered a characteristic expression of contempt, rushed to the fire, and the next minute returned, with her hands full of blazing torches. A few feet from the door there was a bare place, whence the wind had blown the snow, banking it up a short distance off—stooping there, she laid the torches, and bringing more fuel, soon had a bright, clear blaze.

" ' Wolf no come near,' she murmured to herself, ' Wolf 'fraid of burn.'

" By this time the horseman could just be discerned, like a dark shadow in the distance ; he was apparently urging on his steed with both whip and voice, and close behind were the wolves, a most formidable pack, baying, yelling and howling in their ravenous blood-thirstiness.

" On they came, near, still nearer, till the man reined up his steed between the fire and the house. The wolves, frightened by the proximity of fire, the shouts of Webb and the discharge of fire-arms, fell back, and finally slunk away.

" The stranger dismounted, loosened his horses rein and removed his saddle ; the poor beast was well nigh overcome with the fright and labor ; he trembled in every limb, and great drops of sweat rolled off him, while he flung the flecks of foam from his bridle-bits.

" ' Well, stranger, you've had rather a narrow escape,' said Webb, approaching, rifle in hand.

" ' Indeed, I had.'

" There was something in the voice that thrilled through and through me ; I had not seen the man to distinguish his face or features,—but those tones, they awoke a whole world of recollection ; I had returned into the house and lain down, but no bed could hold me then—rising, I went to the door, just in time to hear Webb direct the stranger's attention to the stable, which stood at the end of the house; though separated from it by a narrow yard, I could hear their voices in earnest conversation, and every moment seemed to confirm me more and more in my first impressions. I grew anxious and impatient. Would they never come in? How long they were loitering there. Could I be mistaken? They were coming! I heard their footsteps. In my weakened and enfeebled state, the rush of contending emotions had well nigh overwhelmed me. They came in: I raised my eyes to the face of the stranger—it was indeed the one I had most wished to see; the next instant a dreadful apprehension seized me—a mingled cry of joy and sorrow, of pleasure and apprehension, broke from my lips.

"'My brother! my brother! but where is Tom?'

"Had he not caught me in his arms, I should have fallen to the floor.

"'Why, Ann, is it possible that this is you?' and he held me off at arms length, surveying my form and features.

"'Am I then so changed?'

"'Changed! I should never have known you, my poor, poor sister, how you must have suffered?'

"'Everything but death.'

"Again and again we embraced each other.

"'I had feared never to see you again.'

"'But where is Tom?'

"'Don't ask me, Ann; the subject gives me intense pain.

"'I can guess the reason—he is dead?'

"'He is!'

"'Butchered by the Indians?'

"'Yes! literally butchered; but don't ask me the particulars, don't!' and he made a gesture of putting something terribly painful away from him.

"'How can I help asking you, when he was my own dear brother, and when I should so like to know how and where he died?'

"He paid no attention to what I said, only looked at Webb, and began talking to him of the weather and our prospects of getting back to some civilized settlement. But I would not be put off—I would know the history of his adventures, and where and how my brother died. The arrival of John and the incidents therewith connected, had driven sleep from all our eye-lids. The pain and lameness had also departed from my limbs. Taking my brother's hand, and drawing him to a seat by my side, I asked him to relate the story of his adventures.

"'Not till you answer me one question,' he answered.

"'I will answer a dozen, if you desire it.'

" ' Why is that Indian woman here, are you not afraid of her treachery ? '

" ' Not in the least.'

" We then related how and where we had found her, with the great use she had been to us.

" ' It's probably all right, then,' he answered, and he began his narrative.

" ' You recollect our separation, and the large party of Indians that accompanied us ? '

" I assented.

" ' Well, for some time we travelled due west, by the most fatiguing marches, through a mountainous wilderness; the mounted Indians tied the wretched captives to their saddle-girths, and compelled them to keep up with the horses or be dragged upon the snow. We experienced the most uncomfortable weather, and being thinly clad, our sufferings were terrible. On the third day, the Indians, concluding that there was no danger of pursuit, made preparations to encamp, and began to hunt and reconnoitre the country. Here we remained several days, all the time closely guarded, though it was our policy not to show any uneasiness or desire to escape; our wounds were healed considerably, but the savages were excessively cruel, and seemed to delight in tormenting us. At length some news arrived which frightened them, and they commenced a precipitate removal, plunging still farther into the wilderness. I shall not attempt to describe the horrors of that march, or the sufferings we all endured; we were also made to understand that worse tortures awaited us when we arrived at the Indian villages, hence we determined to escape the first favorable opportunity. It was not long in offering; and one dark night, as we lay in a thick cedar grove, by a large fire, when sleep had locked up their senses, my situation not disposing me to rest, I touched my brother and awoke him; without a word he understood me, and we departed, leaving them to take their rest, and directed our course towards our old home.'

" ' I know just how you must have felt,' I interrupted, 'since I have experienced the same situation.'

" ' I trust your enterprise was not so fool-hardy as ours proved to be,' he answered. 'Even now I blame myself, that we did not wait with more patience for a safer time. The snow afforded them every facility for following our trail; before noon of the next day they came up with us, It would have been utter madness to have resisted them, and so we quietly yielded ourselves into their hands.'

" ' What a dreadful disappointment ! '

" ' We found it something worse. The Indians always resent the attempted escape of a captive as a bitter and deep offence. To fail, is to be subjected to all the horrors of Indian barbarity. We soon found that one or the other was to be made a victim; the fate fell upon Thomas. Don't ask me how he died. Don't! I cannot tell.'

"Covering his face with his hands, his whole frame trembling with excess of emotion, John remained for several minutes in perfect silence, broken only by my sobs; I was weeping—I could not help it. That the fate of my brother had been horrible, I well knew; that the same fate did not await the rest of us, was not by any means certain. At length Webb spoke.

"'It didn't hinder your trying to escape again?' he said.

"'No; it did not.'

"'But the last time you waited until the snow had disappeared, when your trail would be less easily found?' said Webb.

"'I did; nor was this all, I took their fleetest horse; still my way thus far has been beset with dangers, and there can be no safety till the savages are exterminated. We are not in safety here. The light of that fire, which attracted me, might also attract the Indians, have you thought of this?'

"'We thought of it very early in the evening,' I answered, 'But, oh! how glad I am that we let it alone; had it been otherwise, the wolves would most probably have devoured you; your horse could not have held out much longer.'

"'Not a mile farther!'

"'How long had been your race?' asked Webb.

"'It was about dusk, when riding through a dark and lonesome valley, I heard the howl of a wolf—I stopped and listened, thinking that perhaps some Indians were on my track and that this was their signal; I was still more convinced of this, when the sounds were repeated from all quarters of the forest. Of the wolves themselves, I had no fear, but I could not say that of the wild men. Determining to sell my life as dearly as possible, and never be taken alive, (my poor brother's fate had warned me of that,) I rode on; still the sounds grew nearer; my horse soon grew uneasy, snuffed the air, and otherwise manifested the utmost trepidation; all of a sudden, he broke into a fierce gallop, and looking back I could just discern some dark objects moving through the bushes at a short distance.'

"'The wolves?'

"'Of course they were, and now I understood the kind of danger I was to meet. My horse understood it, too, and a steed never behaved more gallantly: it was a terrible race; out we came into the open plain, the pursuers and the pursued. Far ahead, I saw a light faintly glimmering like a star, I knew at once it proceeded from a human habitation, instead of a camp fire in the open air.'

" ' Didn't you fire a rifle ? '

" ' I did; while I was watching the light, a huge black wolf, separated from the rest and sprang at my horse's throat; I placed the muzzle of my rifle almost against the head of the monster, it was so near, and fired: the wolf went down, and for a few minutes the rest of the gang stopped, snapping and snarling at each other, while they tore to pieces and devoured the one I had killed.'

" ' Do you suppose there are Indians in the neighborhood, now ? asked Webb, willing to change the subject.

" ' They cannot be very far off,' was the answer, 'But why do you ask ? '

" 'Because we thought of staying here and resting a few days, your sister there requires it.'

" ' Still, I would not by any means advise it ; the sooner you can get away the better.'

" 'And you will go with us ? ' I asked.

" ' Of course I shall,' he answered.

" 'If we only had a boat ? ' said Webb, 'we might float down the current of the river, and the difficulties and dangers of our journey would be greatly lessened.'

" ' Unless I am greatly mistaken, there is a good boat hidden in a thicket, not ten miles from here.'

" ' And you know where it is ? '

" 'I know where it was.'

" 'We will go and look for it in the morning.'

" 'Why not to-night? I have no inclination to sleep.'

" 'Well, to-night, then.'

" Here I interposed. My brother was just restored to me, and I could not bear to lose sight of him again.

" ' Why not wait till morning, our line of march to-morrow probably lies that way; we can then all go together—if the boat is there, use it, if it is not there, no time will be lost, we can go on without it.'

" This reasoning decided them; it was postponed till the morning.

" When the morning came, we all felt strengthened and refreshed. A comfortable lodging and a warm breakfast had wrought wonders on our frames. How we longed to remain, and durst not, it is impossible to describe. Long and lingering were the looks I cast behind me, as the dwelling receded from view, with only the desolate white waste of snow spread out in front. John had insisted that I should mount his horse, while he walked on foot, and notwithstanding the unfortunate circumstances of our company, and our dangerous situation, as sur-rounded by hostile savages, our meeting so fortunately in the wilderness, made us reciprocally sensible of the utmost satisfaction; at the same time I was painfully conscious that we were then in a most dangerous and helpless situation, exposed daily to perils and death, amongst the savages and wild beasts, in a howling wilderness, many miles from the settlements of white men.

"We traveled this day along the banks of the river, and just at sunset reached the spot where John described the boat as hidden. It was still there, though filled with snow and ice—and as sometime would be required to make it ready, orders were given to encamp for the night in a neighboring ravine. In a deep gorge, a large tree had fallen, surrounded by a dense thicket and hidden from observation by abrupt and precipitous hills; this tree made a convenient position for the back of our camp, logs were placed on the right and left, leaving the front open, where fire might be kindled against another log—while skins, and bark peeled from the basswood, afforded a shelter from the winds and wet.

"The next morning, we perceived that a voyage down the river, if we attempted it, must be attended with great difficulty and much danger. The weather was still cold, though more moderate than heretofore, and the ice on either side of the river, along the margin of the water, was eighteen inches thick: the force of the stream always kept the passage in the centre open; the distance across, between the ice, was about two hundred yards.

"The boat was nothing more than a log canoe, about fifteen feet in length, rounded at both ends, and hollowed with the adze. John assisted by Webb and the Sunny Eye, cleared it of ice, by chopping the frozen water with their tomahawks, and then launched it—an operation exceedingly difficult, though practicable; they dragged it from the shore, over the ice, myself, the wounded man, and all our goods and skins within it, to the water's edge; chopping away the last six or eight feet of unsound ice with their axes, till the head of the canoe was brought close above the water, at a signal from Webb it was pushed off, plump into the stream, a fall of about three feet, and instantly they were all on board, each in his place, and the boat was drifting with the current.

"Our condition, however, was one of great discomfort, as we had no suitable protection from the weather, and were confined to constrained and unnatural postures. Of course, my brother had been obliged to leave his horse, which was no great loss.

"Towards night, and just as we were thinking of going ashore to encamp, we found our passage down the river obstructed by a beaver-dam; numberless large trees had been cut down, near the roots, having apparently been hewn with an axe, and some of them laid directly across the stream—intended, as one might have supposed, as a bridge across it. Here, having fastened our boat, we went ashore, started a fire, and prepared our supper.

"During the night the wolves howled dreadfully, and the distant scream of a panther echoed through the woods; but we began to feel ourselves in comparative safety; we believed that a station of United States troops was not far distant, and we were all aware that the savages would avoid the vicinity of such neighbors.

"The next morning we were up betimes, and though it was a work of time and labor to get the boat across the dam, it was finally accomplished, and we continued down the river for many miles. At length we began to discover signs of civilization that could not be mistaken; we heard the sound of chopping in the woods; the distant lowing of cattle, and the crowing of a cock: then, turning a bend in the stream, a house appeared—not a hut or a cabin, but a good, comfortable house; a woman came to the door and looked at us, her countenance expressive of a strange mixture of surprise and curiosity. Upon going ashore, we were most hospitably received, and after remaining a few days, to recruit our wasted strength, were enabled to join our friends. The Sunny Eye continued with us until the warm weather, when, without a word, she suddenly disappeared."

EASTBURN
NARRATIVE

NARRATIVES OF CAPTIVITIES

THE DANGERS AND SUFFERINGS OF
ROBERT EASTBURN, AND HIS
DELIVERANCE FROM IN-
DIAN CAPTIVITY

REPRINTED FROM THE ORIGINAL EDITION OF 1758
WITH INTRODUCTION AND NOTES BY

JOHN R. SPEARS

CLEVELAND
THE BURROWS BROTHERS COMPANY
1904

CONTENTS

INTRODUCTION

R OBERT EASTBURN, whose *Faithful Narrative* is one of the valuable, because one
of the undoubted, original authorities
relating to the war that destroyed the French
power in North America, was captured by a
force of French soldiers and Indians on a wagon
road that crossed the divide between the Mohawk River and Wood Creek, just north of the
modern city of Rome, New York. He was
carried thence to Canada, where he was adopted
into an Indian family, and where he remained,
part of the time with the Indians, and a part
with the French, for something less than two
years.

It will add to the interest of the narration of
his experiences to know that Eastburn was born
in England in 1710 (see *Memoirs of the Rev.
Joseph Eastburn*), but was brought to America by
his parents when he was four years old. There-
after his home was in Philadelphia. His
parents were Quakers, but in 1739, Robert was
won over to the Presbyterians by the preaching

of George Whitefield,* and when Whitefield organized a congregation, Robert became one of its deacons.

To those who are acquainted with the history of the American frontier during the eighteenth century, the fact that Eastburn was a Christian is of peculiar interest. For when captured by the French invaders he was one of a party of men who were on their way to the frontier post of Oswego to engage in the Indian trade; and no men, as a class, have been so utterly degraded and deeply cursed by their trade as those who have dealt with the aboriginal inhabitants of the earth. With them a thought of fair dealing

---

* Franklin, in his autobiography, says of Whitefield: " In 1739 arrived among us from Ireland the Reverend Mr. Whitefield, who had made himself remarkable there as an itinerant preacher. He was at first permitted to preach in some of our churches; but the clergy, taking a dislike to him, soon refused him their pulpits, and he was obliged to preach in the fields. The multitudes of all sects and denominations that attended his sermons were enormous, and it was matter of speculation to me, who was one of the number, to observe the extraordinary influence of his oratory on his hearers, . . notwithstanding his common abuse of them, by assuring them they were naturally *half beasts and half devils*. It was wonderful to see the change soon made in the manners of our inhabitants. From being thoughtless or indifferent about religion, it seemed as if all the world were growing religious." Under Whitefield's influence a church one hundred feet long by seventy feet broad was erected and paid for before dedication. It was " vested in trustees, expressly for the use of any preacher of any religious persuasion who might desire to say something to the people of Philadelphia."

was an evidence of weakness; the ability to
overreach the savage was their constant boast.

Nevertheless, because some were strictly
honest, according to their light (Quakers and
Moravians traded with the Indians), and because
as a class the traders were most energetic,
enterprising, and courageous, it seems likely
that the story of their work and adventures
should make the most interesting of the chap-
ters of the American annals that have not yet
been written.

Thus, it was the work of the Indian traders
chiefly — their anxiety to preserve and extend
the fur-trade — that caused all the long series
of French and Indian raids on the British-
American frontier during the period so graph-
ically described by Parkman in his *Half Century
of Conflict.* And the first stroke delivered on
the American continent, in what is known as
the "Seven Years' War" — the war during
which Eastburn was captured — was struck by
Charles Langlade, a French trader, with a party
of Ottawas and Ojibways, who attacked the
American traders and the Indians who were
gathered at Pickawillany (near the modern
Piqua, Ohio), June 21, 1752.

To show the courage and enterprise of Robert
Eastburn as a trader, it is necessary to go over
the events that, in America, preceded and led
to the Seven Years' War.

Under the treaty of Utrecht (April 11, 1713), and that of Aix-la-Chapelle (October 7, 1748), the British had the right to trade with the Indians of the interior of North America, regardless of the claims of France to that territory. That every British trader would have made haste to exchange a pint of rum, or six cents' worth of red paint, for a beaver-skin at every opportunity, regardless of treaties, may be admitted; but the fact is they had the legal right to do it.

In pursuit of the profits thus to be obtained, the traders — particularly those of Philadelphia — thronged through the passes of the Alleghanies, after the treaty of Aix-la-Chapelle. In 1749, it is said (Parkman) that three hundred of them led their packhorses into the wilds of the Mississippi Valley. Governor Dinwiddie, of Virginia, said of them that " they appear to be in general a set of abandoned wretches," and Governor Hamilton, of Pennsylvania, concurred in that opinion. But whatever their morals they fearlessly threaded the forests of the region beyond the mountains, met and fought the rival traders of the north, went to the Indian villages wherever to be found, and in time established a station on Sandusky Bay, although the French had a station at Detroit and another on the Maumee River, in northern Ohio.

Commandant Raymond, in charge of the French post on the Maumee, wrote, at about this time:

" All the tribes who go to the English at Pickawillany come back loaded with gifts. . . If the English stay in this country we are lost. We must attack and drive them out."

The Indians that had settled around Detroit were invited to make the attack, but they were found to be " touched with disaffection; " and it was then that Charles Langlade came from the upper lakes and destroyed Pickawillany.

In the meantime the French had taken a formal " renewal of possession " of the Ohio country by sending Céloron de Bienville to bury certain lead plates in the Ohio watershed, and to nail tin plates, on which the French royal coat of arms had been painted, to a number of trees — all of which acts were duly attested by a notary public carried along for the purpose. The attack upon Pickawillany having proved as futile as the expedition of Céloron — though an Indian chief called " Old Britain " was boiled and eaten by Langlade's Indians — measures that were to prove strikingly effective for a time, were adopted by the French.

An expedition was sent by way of Erie, Pennsylvania, to the headwaters of the Alleghany River, where a post was established (1752), and named Le Bœuf. It stood where Waterford,

Pennsylvania, is now found. In the spring of
1753, they moved forward to the site of the
modern Venango, and there prepared to descend
to the junction of the Alleghany and Monongahela in the year after that.

It was now that Governor Dinwiddie, alarmed
at what he deemed an invasion of Virginia, and
at the prospect of a transfer of the horrors of
the French and Indian border warfare from the
frontier of New England to the borders of his
own colony, sent the youthful George Washington to make a formal demand that the French
leave. Legardeur de St. Pierre, commanding
the French, replied, " I do not think myself
obliged to obey."

Accordingly Dinwiddie raised three hundred
" raw recruits," and sent them to occupy the
favorable site for a fort that Washington had
seen, meantime, at the forks of the Ohio.
William Trent, a trader, and a gang of backwoodsmen went with them, and on an unnamed
day in April, 1754, these backwoodsmen began
building a fort where Pittsburg now stands.

Their work was apparently in vain. On April
17th, five hundred Frenchmen, with eighteen
cannon, came down the Alleghany River, under
Captain Claude Pecaudy de Contrecœur, and
drove them away.

Washington's attack on the French force
under Ensign Coulon de Jumonville (May 28,

1754) followed, and that is usually called the beginning, in America, of the Seven Years' War. Then by finesse, rather than by force of arms, the French, under Coulon de Villiers, drove Washington from Fort Necessity (July 4, 1755). Though as yet not formally declared, the great war was well on.

In the meantime (on February 20, of this year), the "trusty and well-beloved Edward Braddock," with two regiments of British soldiers, arrived at Hampton, Virginia. An intercolonial conference was held at Alexandria, beginning on April 14, to consider measures for the prosecution of the war, at which Governor William Shirley, whom Eastburn mentions, was present.

The plans made here included attacks on Acadia, Crown Point, Niagara, and Fort Duquesne, as the post at the forks of the Ohio was called. Shirley " and Dinwiddie stood in the front of the opposition to French designs;" to Shirley was assigned the work of capturing Niagara, and he was placed next in rank to Braddock, in the command of the British forces in America. Braddock himself undertook the task of marching through the wilderness to Fort Duquesne.

How Braddock, with 1,373 picked men, reached Turtle Creek, eight miles from Fort Duquesne, on July 7, crossed the Monongahela on the ninth, and was overwhelmed by an inferior force of

French and Indians on the site of the modern village of Braddock, Pennsylvania, a little later, need not be told here in detail. The important fact is that the French triumph was complete and seemingly decisive. They not only held control of the fort at the forks, but through the shameful retreat of the British to Philadelphia, the French were left in undisputed control of the passes of the Alleghanies.

That the British confirmed their control of Acadia, in this season, by expelling certain French families from the territory; and that the forces under William Johnson checked the French under Baron Dieskau at Lake George, afforded the people of Pennsylvania and Virginia no consolation. For the evil that Governor Dinwiddie had foreseen was upon them. The horrors of the French and Indian wars that, for half a century, had desolated the frontiers of New England, now loomed over the Alleghanies.

" If you consider it necessary to make the Indians to act offensively against the English, his Majesty will approve of your using that expedient," said a letter dated September 6, 1754, from the French colonial minister to Governor Duquesne, of Canada. Duquesne thought that expedient necessary. Captain Dumas succeeded Contrecœur in the command of Fort Duquesne, and on July 24, 1756, wrote to the minister, saying:

" M. de Contrecœur had not been gone a week before I had six or seven different war parties in the field at once, always accompanied by Frenchmen. I have succeeded in ruining the three adjacent provinces, Pennsylvania, Maryland, and Virginia, driving off the inhabitants and totally destroying the settlements over a tract of country thirty leagues wide, reckoning from the line of Fort Cumberland."

And the Rev. Claude Godfroy Coquard, S.J., in a letter to his brother, said in reference to the work of these war parties (*N. Y. Col. MSS.*, vol. x., p. 528):

" The Indians do not make any prisoners; they kill all they meet, men, women, and children. Every day they have some in their kettle, and after having abused the women and maidens, they slaughter or burn them."

On one occasion a band of these Indians swooped down to within sixty miles of Philadelphia. A company of the harassed settlers, in their desperation, came in from the frontier, bringing with them the mutilated bodies of murdered friends and relatives, which they displayed at the doors of the Assembly chamber, while they bitterly cursed the opponents of an active war against the savage intruders.

It was in the midst of the red aggressions of the war parties sent out by Dumas that Robert Eastburn, a deacon in the First Presbyterian

Church of Philadelphia, left home with a party
of traders (among them being his own son, a
lad seventeen years old), and traveled away into
the wilderness, bound to Oswego, the most
advanced post of the American frontier — the
one nearest to the triumphant French — to
engage in the fur-trade with such Indians as he
might find in that region. And he did that,
too, when he knew that Oswego would be in
imminent danger of attack while he was there,
and that there was no small probability that his
party would be intercepted while he was on the
way, as, indeed, actually happened.

Robert Eastburn was, in fact, one of the
many heroes of commerce, now well-nigh forgotten. It was characteristic of such a man to
take his gun and join the soldiers, when a squad
was sent out to hunt the enemy. And no one
is surprised to learn that he was cool enough to
bring down two at one shot, when the enemy
were found.

The story of the fight in which Eastburn was
captured is told, with some variations in the
statements of facts, in volume **x.** of the *New
York Colonial Manuscripts*. The account most
nearly accurate is that in *Journal of Occurances
in Canada from October, 1755, to June, 1756*.
Parkman has the most interesting modern
account in his *Montcalm and Wolfe*.

At the opening of the campaign of 1756, the

French held Ticonderoga, as well as Fort Duquesne, and all the borders of the Great Lakes,
except the one post of Oswego. While yet the
snow lay deep upon the ground in the northern
part of New York, they learned from the Indians
of the Iroquois tribes, who were more or less
friendly to them, that the English contemplated
sending an expedition, by way of Oswego and
Lake Ontario, to attack Niagara, while another
expedition would try to reduce Ticonderoga and
Crown Point. The Indians also told the French
that in pursuance of the English intention to
attack Niagara, immense quantities of provisions had been sent forward toward Oswego,
while the winter roads were good, and that
many of these supplies were piled up in the
storehouses at the carrying-place between the
Mohawk and Wood Creek.

Accordingly Vaudreuil, who had meantime
become governor of Canada, not only did what he
could to strengthen Ticonderoga and Niagara,
but he planned a counter-stroke for the destruction of the forts and stores at the Mohawk-
Wood Creek carrying-place. He also planned
an attack on Oswego, but that was to come later.

To raid the carrying-place, Vaudreuil sent
Joseph Chaussegros de Léry, a distinguished
Canadian officer (Vaudreuil was partial to the
Canadian officers), with three hundred and
sixty-two picked men — soldiers, rangers, and

Indians — from Montreal to the mission of Oswegatchie (now Ogdensburg), and thence by trails through the woods to the head of the Mohawk Valley. After great hardships, due to a lack of provisions and the rigor of the weather (March is a harsh month in the Adirondack region), this force arrived on the road leading from Fort William, at the head of navigation on the Mohawk, to Fort Bull, at the head of navigation on Wood Creek, at 5:30 o'clock on the morning of March 26, 1756. As it happened, they found there a party of twelve teamsters, including an unnamed negro, who were on their way with provisions and traders' goods to Fort Bull. These they attacked, and killed or captured all the party except the negro.

The negro escaped to Fort William and gave the alarm. The French, on questioning their prisoners, under threat of torture, learned that only a small garrison — thirty men — held Fort Bull, and De Léry determined to attack it. Nearly all the Indians in the party objected to this attack, being well satisfied with the plunder obtained from the teamsters, but De Léry, with a little brandy to rouse their courage, persuaded a dozen of them to go with him, and the rest of them to guard the road from Fort William, and then he marched to the attack.

As De Léry approached Fort Bull, some of the Indians whooped, and thus gave the alarm to the garrison, who closed their gate in time to shut out the French, but the French, by a dash forward, were able to secure positions at all the loopholes and prevent the garrison using them. De Léry then called on the garrison to surrender, but in spite of the advantages the French had secured, and in spite of inferior numbers, the heroic band replied with muskets and hand grenades.

The fight lasted for an hour. At the end of that time the French succeeded in chopping down the gate, and as it fell, they rushed in and massacred every person they could find. Two or three escaped death by hiding. The stores were destroyed and the fort was burned.

In the meantime Captain Williams, commanding at Fort William, had sent out a scouting party. Behind this party marched Deacon Eastburn, bearing a musket that had been carefully loaded and primed. And what the result of that movement was, Eastburn shall tell for himself. JOHN R. SPEARS

EASTBURN NARRATIVE

PHILADELPHIA: WILLIAM DUNLAP, 1758

Title-page and text reprinted from a copy of the
original edition in the Library of Congress, Washington, D. C.

A FAITHFUL
NARRATIVE,

OF

The many *Dangers* and *Sufferings*, as well as wonderful *Deliverances* of ROBERT EAST-BURN, during his late *Captivity* among the INDIANS : Together with some *Remarks* upon the *Country* of CANADA, and the *Religion*, and *Policy* of its *Inhabitants* ; the whole intermixed with devout *Reflections*.

By ROBERT EASTBURN.

Published at the earnest REQUEST *of many* FRIENDS, *for the Benefit of the* AUTHOR.

With a recommendatory PREFACE, by the Rev. GILBERT TENNENT.

PSALM 124. 6, 7. *Blessed be the Lord, who hath not given us up as a Prey to their Teeth; our Soul is escaped, as a Bird out of the Snare of the Fowler: The Snare is broken, and we are escaped.*
PSALM 103. 2, 4. *Bless the Lord, O my Soul; and forget not all his Benefits: Who redeemeth thy Life from Destruction; who crowneth thee with loving Kindness, and tender Mercies.*

PHILADELPHIA:
Printed by WILLIAM DUNLAP. 1758.

Preface.

C ANDID READER,
The Author (and Subject) of the enfu-
ing Narrative (who is a Deacon of our
Church, and has been fo for many Years) is of
fuch an eftablifhed good Character, that he
needs no Recommendation of others, where he
is known : a Proof of which, was the general Joy
of the Inhabitants of this City, occafioned by his
Return from a miferable Captivity! Together
with the Readinefs of divers Perfons, to con-
tribute to the Relief of himfelf, and neceffitous
Family, without any Requeft of his, or the leaft
Motion of that Tendency! — But, feeing the following Sheets, are like to fpread into many
Places, where he is not known, permit me to
fay, That upon long Acquaintance, I have found
him to be a Perfon of Candor, Integrity, and
fincere Piety; whofe Teftimony, may with
Safety, be depended upon; which give his Narrative the greater Weight, and may induce to
read it with the greater Pleafure; The Defign
of it is evidently Pious, the Matters contained
in it, and Manner of handling them, will, I

hope, be efteemed by the Impartial, to be enter-
taining and improving: I heartily wifh it may,
by the divine Benediction, be of great and
durable Service.   I am thy fincere Servant, in
the Gofpel of Jefus Chrift.

GILBERT TENNENT.

PHILADELPHIA, *Jan* 19, 1758.

KIND READERS,

On my Return from my Captivity, I had no Thoughts of publifhing any Obfervations of mine to the World, in this Manner; as I had no Opportunity to keep a Journal, and my Memory being broken, and Capacity fmall, I was difinclined to undertake it; but a Number of my Friends were preffing in their Perfwafions, that I fhould do it; with whofe Motion I complied, from a fincere Regard to God, my King, and Country, fo far as I know my own Heart: The following Pages contain, as far as I can remember, the moft material Paffages that happened within the Compafs of my Obfervation, while a Prifoner in Canada; the Facts therein related are certainly true, but the Way of reprefenting fome Things efpecially, is not fo regular, clear, and ftrong, as I could wifh; but I truft it will be fome Apology, that I am not fo much acquainted with Performances of this Kind, as many others; who may be hereby excited to give better Reprefentations of Things, far beyond my Knowledge.

I remain Your unfeigned Well-Wifher,

and humble Servant,

ROBERT EASTBURN.

PHILADELPHIA, *Jan.* 19, 1758.

A Faithful Narrative, &c.

ABOUT Thirty Tradefmen, and myfelf, arrived at Captain Williams's Fort,* (at the Carrying Place) in our Way to Ofwego, the 26th of March, 1756; who informed me, that he was like to be cumbered in the Fort, and therefore advifed us to take the Indian-Houfe for our Lodging. About Ten o'Clock next Day, a Negro Man came running down the Road, and reported, That our Slaymen were all taken by the Enemy; Captain Williams, on hearing this, fent a Serjeant, and about 12 Men, to fee if it was true; I being at the Indian-Houfe, and not thinking myfelf fafe there, in Cafe of an

---

* This fort stood where Rome, New York, now stands. It was erected by Captain William Williams, of Sir William Pepperell's regiment, to guard the south, or Mohawk, end of the carrying-place between the Mohawk River and Wood Creek, in the route from Albany to Oswego. It was a palisaded enclosure with, presumably, a two-story, loopholed loghouse at each of two corners, to give the garrison a commanding view of the enemy, in case of attack. The fort was destroyed by the English after the French captured Oswego, and a little later Fort Stanwix was built in its place, from plans drawn by James Montresor, director of engineers and lieutenant-colonel in the British army in 1758.

Attack, and being alfo fincerely willing to ferve my King and Country, in the beft Manner I could in my prefent Circumftances, afked him if he would take Company? He replied, with all his Heart! Hereupon, I fell into the Rear, with my Arms, and marched after them; when we had advanced about a Quarter of a Mile, we heard a Shot, followed with doleful Cries of a dying Man, which excited me to advance, in order to difcover the Enemy, who I foon perceived were prepared to receive us: In this difficult Situation, feeing a large Pine-Tree near, I repaired to it for Shelter; and while the Enemy were viewing our Party, I having a good Chance of killing two at a Shot, quickly difcharged at them, but could not certainly know what Execution was done, till fome Time after; our Company likewife difcharged, and retreated: Seeing myfelf in Danger of being furrounded, I was obliged to Retreat a different Courfe, and to my great Surprize, fell into a deep Mire, which the Enemy, by following my Track in a light Snow, foon difcovered, and obliged me to furrender, to prevent a cruel Death. (They ftood ready to drive their Darts into my Body, in cafe I refufed to deliver up my Arms.) Prefently after I was taken, I was furrounded by a great Number, who ftripped me of my Cloathing, Hat, and Neckcloth (fo that I had nothing left but a **Flannel Veft**, **without Sleeves**) put a **Rope on my Neck**, bound

my Arms faſt behind me, put a long Band round
my Body, and a large Pack on my Back, ſtruck me
on the Head (a ſevere Blow,) and drove me through
the Woods before them: It is not eaſy to conceive, how diſtreſſing ſuch a Condition is! In the
mean Time, I endeavoured with all my little remaining Strength, to lift up my Eyes to God, from
whom alone I could with Reaſon expect Relief!

Seventeen or Eighteen Priſoners, were ſoon
added to our Number, one of which informed
me, that the Indians were angry with me, and
reported to ſome of their Chiefs, that I had fired
on them, wounded one, and killed another; for
which he doubted they would kill me. Hereupon I conſidered that the Hearts of all Men are
in the Hand of God, and that one Hair of our
Head cannot fall to the Ground without his
Permiſſion: I had not as yet learned what
Numbers the Enemy's Parties conſiſted of; there
being only about 100 Indians who had lain in
Ambuſh on the Road, to kill or take into Captivity all that paſſed between the two Forts.
Here an Interpreter came to me, to enquire
what Strength Capt. Williams had to defend his
Fort? After a ſhort Pauſe, I gave ſuch a diſ-
couraging Anſwer (yet conſiſtent with Truth) as
prevented their attacking it, and of Conſequence
the Effuſion of much Blood; a gracious Providence, which I deſire ever to retain a grateful
Senſe of; for hereby it evidently appeared, that

I was fuffered to fall into the Hands of the
Enemy, to promote the Good of my Countrymen,
to better Purpofe than I could, by continuing
with them; verily the Almighty is wife in
Council, and wonderful in Working.

In the mean Time, the Enemy determined to
deftroy Bull's Fort,* (at the Head of Wood-
Creek) which they foon effected, all being put to
the Sword, except five Perfons, the Fort burnt,
the Provifion and Powder deftroyed; (faving
only a little for their own Ufe) then they retired
to the Woods, and joined their main Body,
which inclufive, confifted of 400 French, and
300 Indians, commanded by one of the principal
Gentlemen † of Quebec; as foon as they got together (having a Prieft with them) they fell on
their Knees, and returned Thanks for their
Victory; an Example this, worthy of Imitation!
an Example which may make prophane pretended Proteftants blufh, (if they are not loft to
all Senfe of Shame) who inftead of acknowl-
edging a God, or Providence, in their military
Undertakings, are continually reproaching him
with Oaths and Curfes; is it any Wonder, that

---

* Fort Bull was a mere palisade wall around store-houses.
It was garrisoned by thirty men from Shirley's regiment. De
Léry attacked it with two hundred and sixty-five men.

† The commander was Joseph Chaussegros de Léry, an
active Canadian officer, who saw service at Fort Duquesne and
Crown Point. He is not to be confounded with Gaspard
Chaussegros de Léry, chief engineer of Canada, who was
called " a great ignoramus."

the Attempts of fuch, are blafted with Difappointment and Difgrace!

The Enemy had feveral wounded Men, both
French and Indians among them, which they
carried on their Backs; befides which, about
Fifteen of their Number were killed, and of us
about Forty: it being by this Time near dark,
and fome Indians drunk, they only marched
about 4 Miles and encamped; the Indians
untied my Arms, cut Hemlock Bowes, and
ftrewed round the Fire, tied my Band to two
Trees, with my Back on the green Bowes, (by
the Fire) covered me with an old Blanket, and
lay down acrofs my Band, on each Side, to prevent my Efcape, while they flept.

Sunday the 28th, rofe early, the Commander
ordered a hafty Retreat towards Canada, for
fear of General Johnfon; * in the mean Time,
one of our Men faid, he underftood the French
and Indians defigned to join a ftrong Party, and
fall on Ofwego,† before our Forces there, could

---

* Sir William Johnson. On learning from the Indians that
the enemy had come to the carrying-place, he hurried rein-
forcements up the Mohawk, but arrived too late to intercept
them.

† Near the end of the seventeenth century Governor Bello-
mont, of New York, suggested that the French might be barred
out of the Iroquois country by building a fort where Oswego,
New York, now stands, but nothing was done in the matter
until Governor Burnet built a " stone house of strength " there,
with his private funds, in the spring of 1727. This house
soon became a noted trading-station, for it proved a formid-

get any Provifion or Succours; having, as they
thought, put a Stop to our relieving them for a
Time: When we encamped in the Evening,
the Commanding-Officer ordered the Indians to
bring me to his Tent, and afked me, by an
Interpreter, If I thought General Johnfon would
follow them, I told him I judged not, but
rather thought he would proceed to Ofwego
(which was indeed my Sentiment, grounded
upon prior Information, and then expreffed to
prevent the Execution of their Defign.) He
farther enquired, what was my Trade? I told
him that of a Smith; he then perfwaded me,
when I got to Canada, to fend for my Wife, ' for
faid he, you can, get a rich Living there;' but
when he faw that he could not prevail, he afked
no more Queftions, but commanded me to return
to my Indian Mafter: Having this Opportunity
of Converfation, I informed the General, that
his Indian Warriors had ftripped me of my
Cloathing, and would be glad he would be good
enough to order me fome Relief; to which he
replied, that I would get Cloaths when I came
to Canada, which was cold Comfort to one
almoft frozen! On my Return, the Indians
perceiving I was unwell, and could not eat their

able rival to the French stations intended to supply the wants
of the Indians on the borders of the Great Lakes. When
Montcalm captured the place (Saturday, August 14, 1756), one
of the defending structures was known on the frontier as Fort
Rascal, because of the character of the work done by its builders.

coarfe Food, ordered fome Chocolate (which
they had brought from the Carrying-Place) to
be boiled for me, and feeing me eat that,
appeared pleafed. A ftrong Guard was kept
every Night; One of our Men being weakened
by his Wounds, and rendered unable to keep
Pace with them, was killed and fcalped on the
Road! — I was all this Time almoft naked, traveling through deep Snow, and wading through
Rivers cold as Ice!

After Seven Days March, we arrived at Lake
Ontario, where I eat fome Horfe-Flefh, which
tafted very agreeably, for to the hungry Man,
as Solomon obferves, every bitter Thing is
fweet (a). The French carried several of their
wounded Men all the Way upon their Backs, and
(many of them wore no Breeches in their Travels

ᵃ On the Friday before we arrived at the Lake, the Indians
killed a Porcupine, which is in bignefs equal to a large Rac-
oon, with fhort Legs, is covered with long Hair, intermixed
with fharp Quills, which are their Defence: It is indeed dangerous coming very near them, becaufe they caft their Quills *
(which are like barbed Irons or Darts) at any Thing that
oppofeth them, which when they peirce, are not eafy to be
drawn out; for, though their Points are fharp and fmooth, they
have a kind of Beard, which makes them ftick faft: However,
the Indians threw it on a large Fire, burnt off the Hair and
Quills, roafted and eat of it, with whom I had a Part.

---

* It is now known that porcupines do not cast or throw their
quills, and are not able to do so, though commonly believed
to do so, at Eastburn's time. Many a backwoodsman has
eaten a porcupine. When young the flesh is as good as that
of a 'possum, they say.

in this cold Seafon, they are ftrong, hardy
Men.) The Indians had Three of their Party
wounded, which they likewife carried on their
Backs, I wifh there was more of this Hardnefs,
fo neceffary for War, in our Nation, which would
open a more encouraging Scene than appears at
prefent! The Prifoners were fo divided, that
but few could Converfe together on our March,
and (which was ftill more difagreeable and
diftreffing) an Indian, who had a large Bunch
of green Scalps, taken off our Men's Heads,
marched before me, and another with a fharp
Spear behind, to drive me after him; by which
Means, the Scalps were very often clofe to my
Face, and as we marched, they frequently every
Day gave the *Dead Shout*,* which was repeated
as many Times, as there were Captives and
Scalps taken! In the Midft of this gloomy
Scene, when I confidered, how many poor Souls
were hurried into a vaft Eternity, with Doubts
of their Unfitnefs for fuch a Change, it made
me lament and expoftulate in the Manner
following; O Sin what haft thou done! what
Defolation and Ruin haft thou brought into this
miferable World? What am I, that I fhould be
thus fpared! My Afflictions are certainly far

---

* Schoolcraft writes *Sa-sa-kuon* to give an idea of the dead
shout. It was the whoop by which the Indians announced,
when approaching a village, their victory, and the number of
scalps and prisoners taken.

lefs than my Sins deferve! Through the exceeding Riches of divine Goodnefs and Grace, I
was in this diftreffing Situation fupported and
comforted, by thefe Paffages of facred Scripture,
viz. That our light Afflictions, which laft but
for a Moment, fhall work for us a far more
exceeding and eternal Weight of Glory. And
that, though no Afflictions are for the prefent
joyous, but grievous; yet neverthelefs, they
afterwards yield the peaceable Fruits of Right-
eoufnefs, to them who are exercifed thereby.
And farther, that all Things fhall work together
for Good, to them that love God; to them who
are the Called, according to his Purpofe. But
to return,

I May, with Juftice and Truth obferve, That
our Enemies leave no Stone unturned to compafs our ruin; they pray, work, and travel to
bring it about, and are unwearied in the Purfuit;
while many among us fleep in a Storm, that has
laid a good Part of our Country defolate, and
threatens the Whole with Deftruction: O may
the Almighty awake us, caufe us to fee our
Danger, before it be too late, and grant us Salvation! O that we may be of good Courage,
and play the Man, for our People, and the
Cities of our God! But alas, I am obliged to
turn my Face towards cold Canada, among
inveterate Enemies, and innumerable Dangers!
O Lord, I pray thee, be my fafe Guard; thou

haſt already covered me in the Hollow of thy Hand; when Death caſt Darts all around me, and many fell on every Side, I beheld thy Salvation!

April 4th, Several French Battoes met us, and brought a large Supply of Proviſion; the Sight of which cauſed great Joy, for we were in great Want; then a Place was ſoon erected to celebrate Maſs in, which being ended, we all went over the Mouth of a River, where it empties itſelf into the Eaſt-End of Lake Ontario, a great Part of our Company ſet off on Foot towards Oſwegotchy; * while the reſt were ordered into Battoes, and carried towards the Entrance of St Lawrence (where that River takes its Beginning) but by reaſon of bad Weather, Wind, Rain, and Snow, whereby the Waters of the Lake were troubled, we were obliged to lie-by, and hall our Battoes on Shore; here I lay on the cold Shore two Days. Tueſday ſet off, and entered the Head of St. Law-

---

* *Oswegotchie.* It was a settlement of Iroquois Indians who had been converted by Abbé Piquet, a French missionary. It was established in 1749 where Ogdensburg, New York, now stands, and it was intended for the promotion of French political and trade interests, as well as the propagation of religion. Piquet called it "La Présentation." In 1753 it contained a palisaded fort, " flanked with block houses; a chapel, a storehouse, a barn, a stable, ovens, a sawmill, broad fields of corn and beans, and three villages of Iroquois, containing in all 49 bark lodges each holding three or four families, . . and as time went on this number was increased."—*Parkman.* The fort was armed with five two-pounder cannon and garrisoned with a squad of French soldiers.

rence, in the Afternoon; came too late at Night, made Fires, but did not lie down to fleep; embarked long before Day, and after fome Miles Progrefs down the River, we faw many Fires on our Right-Hand, which were made by the Men who left us, and went by Land; with them we ftaid till Day, and then again embarked in our Battoes; the Weather was very bad (it fnowed faft all Day) near Night arrived at Ofwegotchy; I was almoft ftarved to Death, but hoped to ftay in this Indian Town till warm Weather; flept in an Indian Wigwam, rofe early in the Morning (being Thurfday) and foon to my Grief difcovered my Difappointment! Several of the Prifoners ¬had Leave to tarry here, but I muft go 200 Miles farther down Stream, to another Indian Town; the Morning being extreamly cold, I applied to a French Merchant (or Trader) for fome old Rags of Cloathing, for I was almoft naked, but to no Purpofe!

About Ten o'Clock, was ordered into a Battoe, on our Way down the River, with 8 or 9 Indians, one of which was the Man wounded in the Skirmifh before mentioned; at Night we went on Shore, the Snow being much deeper than before, we cleared it away, and made a large Fire; here, when the wounded Indian caft his Eyes upon me, his old Grudge revived, he took my Blanket from me, and commanded me to dance round the Fire Bare-foot, and fing the

Prifoners Song, which I utterly refufed; this
furprized one of my fellow Prifoners, who told
me they would put me to Death (for he underftood what they faid) he therefore tried to
perfuade me to comply, but I defired him to let
me alone, and was through great Mercy, enabled
to rejeᶜt his Importunity with Abhorrence!
The Indian alfo continued urging, faying, you
fhall dance and fing; but apprehending my
Compliance finful, I determined to perfift in
declining it at all Adventures, and to leave the
Iffue to the divine Difpofal! The Indian perceiving his Orders difobeyed, was fired with
Indignation, and endeavoured to pufh me into
the Fire, which I leapt over, and he being
weak with his Wounds, and not being affifted
by any of his Brethren, was obliged to defift:
For this gracious Interpofure of Providence, in
preferving me both from Sin and Danger, I
defire to blefs God while I live!

Friday Morning, was almoft perifhed with
Cold. Saturday, proceeded on our Way, and
foon came in Sight of the upper Part of the
Inhabitants of Canada; here I was in great
Hopes of fome Relief, not knowing the Manner
of the Indians, who do not make many Stops
among the French, in their return from War,
till they get Home: However when they came
near fome rapid Falls of Water, one of my
fellow Prifoners, and feveral Indians, together

with myfelf, were put on Shore, to travel by
Land, which pleafed me well, it being much
warmer running on the Snow, than lying ftill
in the Battoe; we paft by feveral French
Houfes, but ftopt at none; the Veffel going
down a rapid Stream, it required hafte to keep
Pace with her, we croffed over a Point of Land,
and found the Battoe waiting for us, as near
the Shore as the Ice would permit: Here we
left St. Lawrence and turned up Conafadauga
River (b) but it being frozen up, we hauled our
Battoe on Shore, and each of us took our Share
of her Loading on our Backs, and marched

ᵇ The River St. Lawrence, at Lake Ontario, takes its Beginning through feveral Iflands, by which we are in no neceffity of
coming within Sight of Frontenac, when we go down the River;
it is fmooth Water from thence to Ofwegotche (or as it is
called by the French *Legalet*) but from hence to Montreal,
the Water is more fwift, with a Number of rapid Streams,
though not dangerous to pafs through with fmall Boats and
Bark Canoes, provided the Stearfmen are careful, and acquainted with the Places. In tranfporting Provifion and
warlike Stores up Stream from Canada to Lake Ontario, there
is a neceffity of unloading Battoes at feveral of the rapid
Streams, and hauling them empty through fhoal Water near
the Shore; and carrying the Loading by Land to where the
Water is more Slack; though there be feveral of thefe Places,
yet the Land Carriage is not very far: The Land on both
Sides the River, appears fertile a great Part of the Way from
the Lake to Montreal; but the nearer the Latter the worfe,
more mirey and ftony: The Timber is White Pine, Afh,
Maple, Beach, Hickory, Hemlock, Spruce; and from the Lake
about 150 Miles down, plenty of White Oak, but none about
Montreal of that Kind.

towards Conafadauga,* an Indian Town, which
was our defigned Port, but could not reach it
that Night; Came to a French Houfe, cold,
weary, and hungry; here my old Friend, the
wounded Indian, again appeared, and related to
the Frenchman, the Affair of my refufing to
dance, who immediately affifted the Indian to
ftrip me of my Flannel Veft, before mentioned,
which was my All: Now they were refolved to
compel me to dance and fing! The Frenchman
was as violent as the Indian, in promoting this
Impofition; but the Women belonging to the
Houfe, feeing the rough Ufage I had, took pity
on me, and refcued me out of their Hands, till
their Heat was over, and prevailed with the
Indian to excufe me from dancing; but he
infifted that I muft be fhaved, and then he would
let me alone (I had at that Time a long Beard,
which the Indians hate) with this Motion I
readily complied, and then the Indian feemed
content.

Sunday, April 11th, Set off towards Conafadauga, traveled about two Hours, and then faw

---

* A mission settlement of Indians containing a village of
Iroquois and another of Algonquins. It was called also the
Lake of the Two Mountains mission. The site is " a point on
the St. Lawrence, just at the [west] extremity of the island
of Montreal, where the river widens into a kind of lake. Two
slight eminences, which soon obtained the name of mountains,
gave it its name. Near these the mission was begun in
1720."— Shea's *American Catholic Missions*.

the Town, over a great River, which was ftill frozen; the Indians ftoped, and we were foon joined with a Number of our own Company, which we had not feen for feveral Days: The Prifoners, in Number Eight, were ordered to lay down our Packs, and be painted; the wounded Indian painted me, and put a Belt of Wampum round my Neck, inftead of the Rope which I had worn 400 Miles. Then fet off towards the Town on the Ice, which was four Miles over; our Heads were not allowed to be covered, left our fine Paint fhould be hid, the Weather in the mean Time very cold, like to Freeze our Ears; after we had advanced nearer to the Town, the Indian Women came out to meet us, and relieved their Hufbands of their Packs.

As foon as we landed at Conafadauga, a large Body of Indians came and incompaffed us round, and ordered the Prifoners to dance and fing the Prifoners Song, (which I was ftill enabled to decline) at the conclufion of which, the Indians gave a Shout, and opened the Ring to let us run, and then fell on us with their Fifts, and knocked feveral down; in the mean Time, one ran before to direct us to an Indian Houfe, which was open, and as foon as we got in, we were beat no more; my Head was fore with beating, and pained me feveral Days. The Squaws were kind to us, gave us boiled Corn and Beans to eat, and Fire to warm us, which

was a great Mercy, for I was both cold and
hungry: This Town lies about 30 Miles North-
Weſt from Montreal, I ſtaid here till the Ice
was gone, which was about Ten Days, and
then was ſent to Cohnewago, in Company with
ſome Indians, who when they came within
Hearing, gave Notice by their Way of ſhouting,
that they had a Priſoner, on which the whole
Town roſe to welcome me, which was the more
diſtreſſing, as there was no other Priſoner in
their Hands; when we came near Shore, a ſtout
Indian took hold of me, and hauled me into the
Water, which was Knee-deep, and very cold: As
ſoon as I got a-ſhore, the Indians gathered round
me, and ordered me to dance and ſing, now
when I was ſtiff with Cold and Wet, and lying
long in the Cannoe; here I only ſtamped to prepare for my Race, and was incompaſſed with
about 500 Indians, who danced and ſung, and at
laſt gave a Shout, and opened the Circle; about
150 young Lads made ready to Pelt me with Dirt
and gravel Stones, and on my ſetting off gave me
a ſtout Volley, without my ſuffering great Hurt;
but an Indian ſeeing me run, met me, and held
me faſt, till the Boys had ſtored themſelves again
with Dirt and ſmall Stones, and let me run; but
then I fared much worſe than before, for a ſmall
Stone among the Mud hit my Right-Eye, and my
Head and Face were ſo covered with Dirt, that I
could ſcarce ſee my Way; but diſcovering a Door

of an Indian Houfe ftanding open, I run in : From
this Retreat I was foon hauled, in order to be
pelted more; but the Indian Women being more
merciful interpofed, took me into a Houfe,
brought me Water to wafh, and gave me boiled
Corn and Beans to eat.   The next Day, I was
brought to the Center of the Town, and cried
according to the Indian Cuftom, in order to be
fent to a Family of Indians, 200 Miles up
Stream, at Ofwegotchy, and there to be adopted,
and abufed no more: To this End, I was delivered to three young Men, who faid I was
their Brother, and fet forward on our Way to
the aforefaid Town, with about 20 more Indians, but by reafon of bad Weather, we were
obliged to encamp on a cold, ftony Shore, three
Days, and then proceeded on; called at Conafadauga, ftaid there about a Week, in which
Time, I went and viewed four Houfes at a
Diftance from the Town, about a Quarter of a
Mile from each other; in which, are reprefented
in large Paint Work, the Sufferings of our Sav-
iour, with Defign to draw the Indians to the
Papift's Religion; the Work is curioufly done:
A little farther ftand three Houfes near together,
on the Top of a high Hill, which they call *Mount
Calvary,** with three large Croffes before them,

---

* Abbé Piquet, who established the mission at Oswegatchie,
erected this Calvary and Way of the Cross. It " is even now
a pilgrimage worthy of attention."—*Shea.*

which compleat the whole Reprefentation: To all thefe Houfes, the Priefts and Indians repair, in performing their grand Proceffions, which takes up much Time (c).

Set off on our Journey for Ofwegotchy, againft a rapid Stream, and being long in it, and our Provifion growing fhort, the Indians put to Shore a little before Night; my Lot was to get Wood, others were ordered to get Fires, and fome to Hunt; our Kettle was put over the Fire with fome pounded Indian Corn, and after it had boiled about two Hours, my oldeft Indian Brother, returned with a She Beaver, big with Young, which he foon cut to Pieces, and threw into the Kettle, together with the Guts, and took the four young Beavers, whole as they came out from the Dam, and put them likewife into

ᶜ The pains the Papifts take to propagate such a bloody and abfurd Religion as theirs, is truly amazing! This brings to my Remembrance, the following Difcourfe, I had with two French Priefts in my Captivity; one of them asked me, if I was a Catholic; apprehending he meant the Romifh Religion, I anfwered no; he replied, *no Bon*. On my relating the above to a fellow Prifoner, he faid, I had anfwered wrong, becaufe by the Word *Catholic* he meant a Chriftian: Some Time after, I was again asked by the other Prieft, if I was a Catholic, I anfwered yes, but not a Roman Catholic; at which he fmiled, and asked, if I was a Lutheran. I replied, no; he again inquired whether I was a Calvanift, I told him I was; to which he faid, with warmth, *no Bon! no Bon!* which fignifieth, it is not good, it is not good. O! may not the Zeal of Papifts, in propagating Superftition and Idolatry, make Proteftants afhamed of their Lukewarmnefs, in promoting the Religion of the Bible!

the Kettle, and when all was well boiled, gave each one of us a large Diſhfull of the Broth, of which we eat freely, and then Part of the old Beaver, the Tail of which was divided equally among us, there being Eight at our Fire; the four young Beavers were cut in the Middle, and each of us got half of a Beaver; I watched an Opportunity to hide my Share (having ſatisfied myſelf before that tender Diſh came to Hand) which if they had ſeen, would have much diſpleaſed them. The other Indians catched young Muſk-Rats, run a Stick through their Bodies, and roaſted, without being ſkinned or gutted, and ſo eat them. Next Morning haſtened on our Journey, which continued ſeveral Days, till we came near Oſwegotchy, where we landed about three Miles from the Town, on the contrary Side of the River; here I was to be adopted, my *Father* and *Mother* that I had never ſeen before were waiting, and ordered me into an Indian Houſe, where we were directed to ſit down ſilent for a conſiderable Time, the Indians appeared very ſad, and my Mother began to cry, and continued crying aloud for ſome Time, and then dried up her Tears, and received me for her Son, and took me over the River to the Indian Town; the next Day I was ordered to go to Maſs with them, but I refuſed once and again, yet they continued their Importunity ſeveral Days, ſaying it was good to go to Maſs, but I ſtill refuſed;

and feeing they could not prevail with me, they
feemed much difpleafed with their new Son (d).
I was then fent over the River, to be employed
in hard Labour, as a Punifhment for not going
to Mafs, and not allowed a Sight of, or any Converfation with my fellow Prifoners; the old
Indian Man that I was ordered to work with,
had a Wife, and fome Children, he took me into
the Woods with him, and made Signs that I
muft chop, giving me an Ax, the Indian foon
faw that I could handle the Ax: Here I tried to
reconcile myfelf to this Employ, that they might
have no Occafion againft me, except concerning
the Law of my God; the old Man began to
appear kind, and his Wife gave me Milk and
Bread when we came Home, and when fhe got
Fifh, gave me the Gills to eat, out of real Kindnefs; but perceiving I did not like them, gave
me my own choice, and behaved lovingly!
Here I faw that God could make Friends of

d When I was at Ofwegotchy, the Indians took Notice, that I
frequently retired alone, and fuppofing I had fome bad Defign,
threatened if I did not defift, they would Tomahawk me; but
my fellow Prifoner, who underftood their Language, told them
it would be a pity to hurt me on that Account, for I only went
into a private Place to pray, which was true; the Indians
replied, if fo, it was good; but being yet fufpicious, took Pains,
by watching to find out how the Cafe was, and when they
fatisfied themfelves, feemed pleafed! and did not offer to
interrupt me any more, which was a great Mercy; as the
Contrary would have in fome Degree, marred my Converfe
with God.

cruel Enemies, as he once turned the Heart of angry Efau into Love and Tendernefs; when we had finifhed our Fence, which had employed us about a Week, I fhewed the old Squaw my Shirt (having worn it from the Time I was firft taken Prifoner, which was about feven Weeks) all in Rags, Dirt, and Lice; fhe faid it was not good, and brought me a new One, with ruffled Sleeves (faying that is good) which I thankfully accepted. The next Day they carried me back to the Indian Town, and admitted me to converfe with my fellow Prifoners, who told me we were all to be fent to Montreal, which accordingly came to pafs.

Montreal, at our Arrival here, we had our Lodging firft in the Jefuit's Convent, where I faw a great Number of Priefts, and People that came to Confeffion; after fome ftay, we were ordered to attend, with the Indians, at a Grand Council, held before the head General Vaudriel;* we Prifoners fat in our Rank (furrounded with our Fathers and Brethren) but were afked no Queftions: the General had a Number of Officers to attend him in Council, where a noted Prieft, called Picket,† fat at his Right-Hand,

---

* Pierre François de Rigaud, Marquis de Vaudreuil-Cavagnal. He was governor of Canada from the summer of 1755 till the French lost the country, 1759.

† Abbé François Piquet. He was one of the most patriotic and zealous priests in French America. Though best known as the founder of Oswegatchie, his work at the Lake of the

who underftands the Indian Tongue well, and
does more Hurt to the Englifh, than any other
of his Order in Canada (his Dwelling is at
Ofwegotchy).   Here I was informed that fome
Meafures were concerted to deftroy Ofwego,
which they had been long preparing to execute;
we in our Journey met many Battoes going up
Stream, with Provifion and Men for an Attack
on our Frontiers, which confirmed the Report:
The Council adjourned to another Day, and then
broke up.   My Indian Father and Mother took
me with them to feveral of their old Acquaintance, who were French, to fhew them their
lately adopted Son; thefe Perfons had been
concerned with my Father and other Indians,
in deftroying many Englifh Families in their
younger Days; and (as one ftanding by who
underftood their Language, faid,) were boafting
of their former Murders!   After fome Days the
Council was again called, before which, feveral
of the Oneida Chiefs appeared, and offered fome
Complaint againft the French's attacking our
Carrying-Place, it being their Land; but the

Two Mountains was notable in the annals of the Church. He
was stationed at Fort Frontenac, at one time. When Montcalm captured Oswego, Piquet was present, and erected a
huge cross to commemorate the French victory. He accompanied a number of raiding parties that invaded the British
settlements. His energy was untiring. Though called vain
and boastful, it is certain that he was ever ready to back his
words with deeds.

General laboured to make them eafy, and gave them fundry Prefents of Value, which they accepted (e): After which, I knowing thefe Indians were acquainted with Captain Williams, at the Carrying-Place, fent a Letter by them, to let my Family and Friends know I was yet alive, and longed for Redemption; but it never came to Hand. The Treaty being ended, the General fent about ten Gallons of red Wine to the Indians, which they divided among us; after

---

˙ The French in Canada, well knowing the great Importance of having the Indians in their Intereft, to promote their ambitious and unjuft Defigns, ufe a variety of Methods with them, among which, the following one is excellent in itfelf, and well worthy of Imitation, viz. They are exceeding careful to prevent fpirituous Liquors being fold to the Indians, and if any of the Inhabitants are proved guilty of it, their temporal Intereft is quite broke, and corporal Punifhment inflicted on them; unlefs the General, on fome particular Occafion, orders his Commiffioners to deliver fome to them. I may add, that knowing their Number is fmall, compared with the Britifh Inhabitants on this Continent, and muft quickly fall into their Hands, in cafe we united, and entered boldly into the Heart of their Country with a fufficient Force; for that very Reafon, they choofe to keep us continually on the Defencive, by fending when Occafion requires, large Bodies of Regulars, together with great Numbers of Indians, upon long and tedious Marches, that we may not come near their Borders; and efpecially by employing the Latter, conftantly to wafte and ravage our Frontiers, by which we are murdered by Inches, and beat without a Battle! By what I could learn when I was among them, they do not fear our Numbers, becaufe of our unhappy Divifions, which they deride, and from them, ftrongly expect to conquer us entirely! which may a gracious God, in Mercy, prevent!

came the Prefents, confifting of Coats, Blankets,
Shirts, Skins (to make Indian Shoes) Cloth (to
make Stockings) Powder, Lead, Shot, and to
each a Bag of Paint, for their own Ufe, &c.
After we Prifoners had our Share, my Mother
came to me with an Interpreter, and told me I
might ftay in the Town, at a Place fhe had
found for me, if I pleafed (this was doubtlefs
the Confequence of my declining to obey her
Orders, in fome Inftances that affected my
Confcience) this Propofal I almoft agreed to;
but one of my fellow Prifoners, with whom I
had before fome Difcourfe, about making our
Efcape from the Indian Town, oppofed the
Motion, and faid, '' pray do not ftay, for if you
do, we fhall not be able to form a Plan for our
Deliverance; '' on which I told her I chofe to
go Home with her, and foon fet off by Land in
our Way thither, to Lafcheen,* diftant from

---

* La Chine was the name given by envious competitors to
the frontier trading-post, established by La Salle, soon after
his arrival (1666) in New France.   It stood at the head of the
rapids above and nine miles from Montreal.   It was the most
dangerous, and probably it was then the most profitable post
in America.   Having learned from Seneca Indians that a river
heading in their country flowed to a great salt sea, far away
to the south, La Salle supposed it emptied into the South Sea,
and that he might, by following that route, reach China.
With unsurpassed courage and enterprise he mortgaged his
trading-post, though it was yielding him large profits, to raise
funds for the exploration of this river.   He succeeded in following it as far as the falls of the Ohio (Louisville, Kentucky),
and then, because his men deserted him, he was obliged to

Montreal about 9 Miles, where we left our
Cannoes, and then proceeded, without Delay, on
our Journey; in which I faw, to my Sorrow,
great Numbers of Soldiers, and much Provi-
fions, in Motion towards Lake Ontario.

After a painful and diftreffing Journey, we
arrived at Ofwegotchy, where we likewife faw
many Battoes, with Provifion and Soldiers,
daily paffing by in their Way to Frontenac,*
which greatly diftreffed me for Ofwego! Hence
I refolved, if poffible, to give our People Notice
of their Danger: To this End, I told two of
my fellow Prifoners, that it was not a Time to
fleep, and afked if they would go with me, to
this they heartily agreed; but we had no Provifion, were clofely eyed by the Enemy, and
could not lay up a Stock out of our Allowance:
However, at this Time, Mr. Picket (before mentioned) had concluded to dig a large Trench
round the Town; I therefore went to a Negro,

---

return, ruined, to Montreal. He had gone to find China; he
returned to find the mortgage on his post at the rapids fore-
closed. His old rivals, to deride him, began to call his lost
post China — *La Chine* — and the name remains to this day,
perpetuating the story of La Salle's first expedition into the
wilds of America, and the ill nature of his competitors.

*Frontenac was the name (called also Cataraqui) of the
fort, trading-post, and settlement established (1673) by La
Salle and Count de Frontenac, where Kingston, Ontario, now
stands. It was the first of the chain of forts intended to
extend from Montreal to New Orleans that La Salle planned
to secure the interior of the continent to the French crown.

the principal Manager of this Work (who could ſpeak Engliſh, French, and Indian, well) and aſked him, if he could get Employ for two others, and myſelf, which he ſoon did; for which we were to have Meat and Wages. Here we had a Proſpect of procuring Proviſion for our Flight; this, I in ſome Time effected for myſelf, and then aſked my Brethren if they were ready, who replied they were not yet, but ſaid, Ann Bowman, our fellow Priſoner, had brought 130 Dollars from Bull's Fort, and would give them all they had Need of; I told them it was not ſafe to diſcloſe ſuch a Secret to her, but they blamed me for my Fears, and applied to her for Proviſion, letting her know our Intention, who immediately informed the Prieſt of it; on which we were apprehended, the Indians appriſed of our Deſign, and a Court called; by Order of which, four of us were confined under a ſtrong Guard, in a Room within the Fort, for ſeveral Days.

From hence, another and myſelf were ſent to Cohnewago, under a ſtrong Guard of 60 Indians, to prevent my ploting any more againſt the French, and baniſh all Hope of my Eſcape! However, when we arrived at this Place, it pleaſed that gracious God, who has the Hearts of all Creatures in his Hand, to incline the Captain of the Guard, to ſhew me great Kindneſs, in giving me Liberty to walk or work where I pleaſed, within any ſmall Diſtance; on which

I went to work with a French Smith, for fix
Livers and five Soufe per Week; which the Captain let me have to myfelf, and farther favoured
me with the Priviledge of Lodging at his Mother's
Houfe, an Englifh Woman (named Mary Harris,* taken Captive when a Child, from Dear-
field, in New-England) who told me fhe was my
Grand-mother, and was kind; but the Wages
being fmall, and not fufficient to procure fuch
Cloathing as I was in Want of, I proceeded no
farther with the French Smith, but went to my
Uncle Peter, and told him I wanted Cloaths, and
that it would be better to let me go to Montreal,
and work there, where I could Cloath myfelf
better, than by ftaying with him, and that without any Charge to him, who after fome Reafoning
confented.

Set off on my Journey to Montreal, and on
my entring the City met an Englifh Smith,
who took me to work with him; after fome
Time, we fettled to work in a Shop, oppofite to
the General's Door, where we had the Opportunity of feeing a great Part of the Forces of
Canada (both Soldiers and Indians) who were
commonly brought there, before their going
out to War; and likewife all Prifoners, by which

---

* Mary Harris was one of a considerable number of captured
New England children who learned to prefer the Indian way
of living to that of civilized people. According to Parkman,
a tributary of the Muskingum River, in Ohio, was named
White Woman's Creek, in her honor.

Means we got Intelligence how our People were preparing for Defence; but no good News from Ofwego, which made me fear, knowing that great Numbers of French were gone againft it, and hearing of but few to defend it. Prayers were put up in all the Churches of Canada, and great Proceffions made, in order to procure Succefs to their Arms, againft poor Ofwego; but our People knew little of their Danger, till it was too late: Certainly if more frequent and earneft Application (both in private and public) was made to the God of Battle, we might with greater Probability, expect Succefs would crown our military Attempts! To my Surprize, the difmal News came, that the French had taken one of the Ofwego Forts; in a few Hours, in Confirmation of this, I faw the Englifh Standards (the melancholly Trophy of Victory) and the French rejoicing at our downfal, and mocking us poor Prifoners, in our Exile and Extremity, which was no great Argument either of Humanity, or true Greatnefs of Mind; great Joy appeared in all their Faces, which they expreffed by loud Shouts, firing of Cannon, and returning Thanks in their Churches; but our Faces were covered with Shame, and our Hearts filled with Grief! - - Soon after, I faw feveral of the Officers brought in Prifoners, in fmall Parties, and the Soldiers in the fame Manner, and confined within the Walls, in a ftarving Condi-

tion, in order to make them Work, which fome
complied with, but others bravely refufed; and
laft of all came the Tradefmen, among whom
was my Son, who looking round faw his Father,
who he thought had long been dead; this joyful
Sight fo affected him, that he wept! — nor could
I, in feeing my Son, remain unconcerned! —
no; the Tendernefs of a Father's Bowels, upon fo
extraordinary an Occafion, I am not able to
exprefs, and therefore muft cover it with a Vail
of Silence! — But he, with all my Philadelphia
Friends, being guarded by Soldiers, with fixed
Bayonets, we could not come near each other,
they were fent to the common Pound; but I
haftened to the Interpreter, to try if I could get
my Child at Liberty, which was foon effected!
When we had the Happinefs of an Interview,
he gave me fome Information of the State of
our Family, and told me, as foon as the News
were fent Home, that I was killed, or taken, his
Mother was not allowed any more Support from
my Wages, which grieved me much, and added
to my other Afflictions (f)!

ᶠ In the mean Time, it gave me fome Pleafure, in this Situation, to fee an Expreffion of equal Duty and Prudence in my
Sons Conduct, who, though young in Years (about 17) and in
fuch a confufed State of Things, had taken care to bring, with
much Labour and Fatigue, a large Bundle of confiderable
Value to me, it being Cloathing, &c. which I was in great Need
of; he likewife faved a Quantity of Wampum, which we
brought from New-York, and afterwards fold here, for 150
Livers. He traveled with me Part of the Journey towards

When the People taken at Ofwego, were fetting out on their Way to Quebec, I made Application for Liberty to go with them; but the Interpreter replied, that I was an Indian Prifoner, and the General would not fuffer it, till the Indians were fatisfied; and as they lived Two Hundred Miles from Montreal, it could not be done at that Time: Finding that all Arguments, farther on that Head, would not avail, becaufe I was not included in the Capitulation; I told the Interpreter, my Son muft go and leave me! in order to be ready at Quebec to go Home, when the Ofwego People went, which probably would be foon; he replied, " It would

Ofwego, but not being fo far on his Way, as I was when taken, he did not then fall into the Enemy's Hands, but continued free till Ofwego was taken, and was then remarkably delivered from the Hands of the Indians, in the following Manner, 15 young Lads were drafted out to be delivered to them (which from their known Cuftom, it is reafonable to conclude, was to fill up the Number they had loft in the Battle *) among which he was one: This barbarous Defign, which is contrary to the Laws of War, among all civilized Nations, the French artfully concealed, under the Pretext of fending them to work in the Battoes; but my Child taking Notice, that all that were chofen were fmall Lads, doubted their real Intention was bad,

---

* In Delafield's biography of Francis Lewis (one of the prisoners captured at Oswego) is this paragraph (p. 20): " Montcalm allowed his Indian allies to select thirty prisoners as their share of the booty, and Lewis was one of the number. The Indians retreated northward. Toward the close of each day when they found . . a pleasant spot which invited them to rest and feast, they lit their fires and celebrated their victory by the sacrifice of a captive."

be better to keep him with me, for he might be a Mean to get me clear much fooner."

The Officers belonging to Ofwego, would gladly have had me with them, but found it impracticable; this is an Inftance of Kindnefs and Condefcenfion, for which I am obliged! Captain Bradley, gave me a good Coat, Veft, and Shirt; and a young Gentleman, who formerly lived in Philadelphia, gave four Piftoles (his Name is James Stone, he was Doctor at Ofwego). Thefe generous Expreffions of Kindnefs and Humanity, I am under great Obligations to remember with affectionate Gratitude, and if ever it be in the Compafs of my Power,

---

and therefore flipt out of his Rank and concealed himfelf, by which Means, under God, he was preferved from a State of perpetual Captivity; his Place being filled up in his Abfence, the other unhappy Youths were delivered up a Sacrifice to the Indian Enemy, to be inftructed in Popifh Principles, and employed in Murdering their Countrymen; yea, perhaps, their Fathers and Brethren, O horrible! O lamentable! How can the French be guilty in cold Blood, of fuch prodigious Iniquity? Befides their infatiable Thirft of Empire, Doubtlefs the Pardons they get from their Pope, and their Priefts, embolden them, which brings to my Mind, what I faw when among them: On a Sabbaoth Day, perceiving a great Concourfe of People at a Chapel, built on the Commons, at fome Diftance from the City, I went to fee what was the Occafion, and found a kind of a Fair, at which were fold Cakes, Wine, Brandy, &c. I likewife faw many Carts and Chafes attending, the Chapel Doors in the mean Time open, Numbers of People going in and out, and a Board hanging over the Door, on which was written, in large Letters, INDULGENCE PLENARY, or FULL PARDON.

to requite: This Money, together with what my
Son brought, I was in Hopes would go far towards
procuring my Releafe, from my Indian Mafters;
but feeing a Number of Prifoners in fore Diftrefs,
among which were, the Captains Grant and
Shepherd,* and about Seven more in Company,
I thought it my Duty to relieve them, and com-
mit my Releafe to the Difpofal of Providence!
Nor was this fuffered to turn to my Difadvantage
in the Iffue, for my Deliverance was brought
about in due Time, in another, and unexpected
Way. This Company informed me of their
Intention to Efcape, accordingly I gave them
all the Help in my Power, faw them clear of
the Town, on a Saturday Evening, before the
Centries were fet at the Gates, and advifed them
not to part from each other, and delivered to
Captain Shepherd two Pocket Compaffes; but
they contrary to this Counfel parted, and faw
each other no more: By their feparating, Captain Grant, and Serjeant Newel, were deprived
of the Benefit of a Compafs; the other Part got
fafe to Fort William Henry, as I was informed
by Serjeant Henry, who was brought in Prifoner, being taken in a Battle, when gallant, inde-
fatigable Captain Rogers, made a brave Stand,

* Shepard was picked up by a scouting party that was under
the active Major Robert Rogers. They had gone down Lake
George on skates to look after French stragglers and examine
the French posts.

againſt more than twice his Number! But I
have not heard any Account of Captain Grant!
Was enabled, through much Mercy, to continue
communicating ſome Relief to other Priſoners,
out of the Wages I received for my Labour,
which was 40 Livers per Month!

In the latter Part of the Winter, Coal and Iron
were ſo ſcarce, that I was hard ſet to get any
more Work; I then offered to work for my Diet
and Lodging, rather than be thruſt into a ſtink-
ing Dungeon, or ſent among the Indians: The
Interpreter took ſome Pains (which I thankfully
acknowledge) but without Succeſs; however,
as I offered to work without Wages, a Frenchman took me and my Son in, upon theſe Terms,
till a better Birth preſented; here we ſtaid one
Week, but heard of no other Place, then he
offered me and my Son, 30 Livers per Month,
to ſtrike and blow the Bellows, which I did for
about two Months, and then was diſcharged,
and traveled about from Place to Place, having
no fixed Abode, and was obliged to lay out the
ſmall Remains of my Caſh, in buying a little
Victuals, and took a Hay-Loft for my Lodging:
I then made my Caſe known to the kind Interpreter, and requeſted him to conſider of ſome
Means for my Relief, who replied he would;
in the mean Time, as I was taking a walk in
the City, I met an Indian Priſoner, that belonged to the Town where my Father lived,

who reported, that a great Part of the Indians there, were juft come, with a Refolution to carry me back with them; and knowing him to be a very honeft Fellow, I believed the Truth of it, and fled from the Town to be concealed from the Indians; in the mean while, Schemes were formed for an Efcape, and well profecuted: The Iffue of which was fortunate. General Vaudriel, gave me and my Son, Liberty (under his Hand) to go to Quebec, and work there at our Pleafure, without Confinement, as Prifoners of War; by which Means, I was freed from paying a Ranfom.

The Commiffary, Monfieur Partwe, being about to fet off for Quebec, my Son informed me that I muft come to Town in the Evening, a Paffage being provided for us; I waited till near Dark, and then entered the Town, with great Care, to efcape the Indians, who kept watch for me (and had done fo for fome Time) which made it very difficult and dangerous to move; however, as they had no Knowledge of my Son, he could watch their Motions, without their Sufpicion (the Providence of God is a great Deep, this Help was provided for my Extremity, not only beyond my Expectation, but contrary to my Defign.) In the Morning, upon feeing an Indian fet to watch for me, over againft the Houfe I was in, I quickly made my Efcape, through the back Part of the Houfe, over fome high Pickets, and out of the City, to the River Side, and fled!

A Friend knowing my Scheme for Deliverance,
kindly affifted me to conceal myfelf: The Commiffary had by this Time got ready for his
Voyage, of which my Son giving me Notice, I
immediately, with no lingering Motion, repaired
to the Boat, was received on board, fet off quite
undifcovered, and faw the Indians no more!
A very narrow and furprizing Efcape, from a
violent Death! (For they had determined to kill
me, in cafe I ever attempted to leave them)
which lays me under the ftrongeft Obligations,
to improve a Life refcued from the Jaws of fo
many Deaths, to the Honour of my gracious
Benefactor! — But to return, the Commiffary,
upon feeing the Difmiffion I had from the General, treated us courteoufly! (g)

Arrived at Quebec, May 1ft, The honorable
Colonel *Peter Schuyler*,* hearing of my coming

g Saw many Houfes and Villages in our Pafs along the River
St. Lawrence towards the Metropolis; and here it may be
with Juftice obferved, that the Inhabitants of Canada in general, are principally (if not wholly) fettled upon Rivers, by
reafon that their back Lands being flat and fwampy, are
therefore unfit to bear Grain: Their Wheat is fown in the
Spring of the Year, becaufe the Winter is long, and would
drown it; they feem to have no good Notion of making
Meadow (fo far as I had an Opportunity of obferving) their
horned Cattle are few and poor, their Living in general mean,
they eat but little Flefh, neverthelefs they are ftrong and hardy.

* Colonel Peter Schuyler. He was the son of Arent Schuyler, and both were notable men in the British colonies. The
colonel was in command of a New Jersey regiment at Oswego
when the French captured the place. " While a prisoner in

there, kindly fent for me, and after enquiries about my Welfare, &c. generoufly told me I fhould be fupplied, and need not trouble myfelf for Support! This public fpirited Gentleman, who is indeed an Honour to his Country, did in like Manner, nobly relieve many other poor Prifoners at Quebec! — Here I had full Liberty to walk where I pleafed, and view the City, which is well fituated for Strength, but far from being impregnable.

Here, I hope, it will not be judged improper, to give a fhort Hint of the French Governor's Conduct; even in Time of Peace, he gives the Indians great Encouragement to Murder and Captivate the poor Inhabitants on our Frontiers; an honeft, good Man, named William Rofs, was taken Prifoner twice in the Time of Peace; when he was firft taken, he learned a little of the French Tongue, was after fome Time redeemed, and got to his Place of Abode: Yet fome Years after, he, with two Sons, was again taken, and brought to Quebec; the Governor feeing the poor Man was Lame, and one of his Legs fmaller than the other, reproved the In-

---

Canada he kept open house for the relief of his fellow sufferers, and gave large sums to the Indians for the redemption of captives; many of whom he afterwards, at his own expense, maintained while there, and provided for their return, trusting to their abilities and honor for repayment; and lost considerable that way, but seemed to think it money well bestowed." He lived at No. 1 Broadway, New York City, at one time.

dians for not killing him, afking, " what they brought a lame Man there for, who could do nothing but eat; you fhould, faid he, have brought his Scalp!'' However, another of his Countrymen, more merciful than his Excellency, knowing the poor Prifoner to be a quiet, hard-working Man, redeemed him from the Indians; and two other Frenchmen bought his two Sons: Here they had been Slaves more than three Years, when I firft arrived at Quebec; this Account I had from Mr. Rofs himfelf, who farther added, that the Governor gave the Indians Prefents, to encourage them to proceed, in that kind of Work, which is a Scandal to any civilized Nation, and what many Pagans would abhor! Here alfo, I faw one Mr. Johnfon, who was taken in a Time of Peace, with his Wife, and three fmall Children (his Wife was big with Child of a Fourth, and delivered on the Road to Canada, which fhe called Captive *) all which, had been Prifoners between three and four Years, feveral young Men, and his Wife's Sifter, were likewife taken Captive with them, and made Slaves!

---

* Parkman refers to the daughter of John Smead and wife, as a child that was named " Captivity " under similar circumstances. The Smeads were captured when Fort Massachusetts was destroyed (1746). The child was born while they traveled through the woods. The Indians made a litter of poles and deerskins, placed mother and child on it, covered them with a bearskin, and then carried them on their way to the settlement in Canada.

Our Cartel being ready, I obtained Liberty to go to England in her; we fet Sail the 23d of July, 1757, in the Morning, and difcharged our Pilot about 4 o'Clock in the Afternoon; after which, we neither caft Anchor or Lead, till we got clear of the great River St. Lawrence, from which, I conclude, the Navigation is much fafer than the French have reported; in 28 Days we arrived at Plymouth, which occafioned great Joy, for we were ragged, lowfy, fick, and in a Manner, ftarved; and many of the Prifoners, who in all were about 300 in Number, were fick of the Small-Pox: My Son and Self, having each a Blanket Coat (which we bought in Canada to keep us warm) and now expecting Relief, gave them to two poor fick Men, almoft naked! But as we were not allowed to go on Shore, but removed to a King's Ship, and fent to Portf-mouth, where we were ftill confined on board, near two Weeks, and then removed to the Mer-maid,* to be fent to Bofton; we now repented our well ment, though rafh Charity, in giving

---

* According to Allen's *Battles of the British Navy* the " Mermaid " was a 28-gun frigate. During our war of the Revolution the " Mermaid " fell in with the fleet under Count D'Estaing, as it was sailing up the American coast to attack General Howe, who was then (1778) in Philadelphia. The fleet went in chase of the " Mermaid," and drove her ashore on Cape Henlopen, but were thereby so much delayed in what was already an overlong passage, that Howe, and such few ships as were at Philadelphia, got clear of the Delaware.

our Coats away, as we were not to get any more, all Application to the Captain for any Kind of Covering being in vain; our Joy was turned into Sorrow, at the Profpeᶜt of coming on a cold Coaſt, in the Beginning of Winter, almoſt naked, which was not a little increaſed, by a near View of our *Mother Country*, the Soil and Comforts of which, we were not ſuffered to touch or taſte (h).

September the 6th, Set Sail for Boſton, with a Fleet in Convoy, at which we arrived on the Seventh of November, in the Evening; it being Dark, and we Strangers, and poor, it was difficult to get a Lodging (I had no Shoes, and but Pieces

----

ʰ On board the Mermaid Man of War, being in a diſtreſſed Condition, and hearing little from the Mouths of many of my Countrymen, but Oaths and Curſes (which much increaſed my Afflicᵗion) and finding it difficult to get a retired Place, I crept down into the Hold among the Water Casks, to cry to God; here the Lord was gracviouſly pleaſed to meet with me, and give me a Senſe of his fatherly Love and Care; here he enabled me (bleſſed be his Name for ever) to look back and view how he had led me, and guarded me with a watchful Eye and ſtrong Arm, and what Pains he had taken to wean me from an over-love of time Things, and make me content that he ſhould chooſe for me: Here I was enabled to ſee his great Goodneſs in all my Diſappointments, and that Afflicᵗions were not Evidences of God's Wrath, but the Contrary, to all that honeſtly Endeavour to ſeek him with Faith and Love; here I could ſay, God is worthy to be ſerved, loved, and obeyed, though it be attended with many Miſeries in this World! What I have here mentioned, ſo far as I know my heart, is neither to exalt myſelf, or offend any one upon Earth, but to glorify God, for his Goodneſs and Faithfulneſs to the Meaneſt of his Servants, and to encourage others to truſt in him!

of Stockings, and the Weather in the mean
Time very Cold) we were indeed directed to
a Tavern, but found cold Entertainment there,
the Mafter of the Houfe feeing a ragged and
lowfy Company, turned us out to Wander in the
Dark; he was fufpicious of us, and feared we
came from Halifax, where the Small-Pox then
was, and told us, he was ordered not to receive
fuch as came from thence: We foon met a
young Man, who faid he could find a Lodging
for us, but ftill detained us by afking many
Queftions; on which I told him we were in no
Condition to Anfwer, till we came to a proper
Place, which he quickly found, where we were
ufed well; but as we were lowfy, could not
expect Beds. The next Morning, we made
Application for Cloathing; Mr. Erwing, Son-in-
Law to the late General Shirley,* gave us Relief,

---

* William Shirley was governor of Massachusetts when this
war began.   After the conference with Braddock in Virginia
Shirley was placed in command of the expedition that was to
reduce Niagara.   At Braddock's death he became commander-
in-chief of the British forces in America, and he held that
position at the time Eastburn was captured.   It was by his
orders that Fort Bull was filled with supplies, though but
poorly garrisoned to resist a French invasion.   He was an
earnest, energetic, and capable civil officer, but was most unfortunate in this war, for his military enterprises failed, and
he lost two sons in the army.   Franklin in his autobiography
says of him: "Tho' Shirley was not a bred soldier, he was
sensible and sagacious in himself, and attentive to good advice
from others, capable of forming judicious plans, and quick
and active in carrying them into execution."

not only in refpect of Apparel, but alfo Three
Dollars per Man, to bear our Charges to Newport: When I put on frefh Cloaths, I was feized
with a cold Fit, which was followed by a high
Fever, and in that Condition obliged to Travel
on Foot, as far as Providence, in our Way to
Rhode-Ifland (our Money not being fufficient to
hire any Carriage, and find us what was needful
for Support:) In this Journey, I was exceedingly diftreffed! Our Comforts in this Life,
are often allaved with Miferies, which are
doubtlefs great Mercies when fuitably improved;
at Newport, met with Captain Gibbs, and agreed
with him for our Paffage to New-York, where
we arrived, November 21ft, met with many
Friends, who expreffed much Satisfaction at
our Return, and treated us kindly, particularly
Meffrs. Livingfton, and Waldron.

November 26th, 1757. Arrived at Philadelphia, to the great Joy of all my Friends, and
particularly of my poor afflicted Wife and
Family, who thought they fhould never fee me
again, till we met beyond the Grave; being
returned, fick and weak in Body, and empty-
handed, not having any Thing for my Family's
and my own Support, feveral humane and generous Perfons, of different Denominations, in
this City (without any Application of mine,
directly or indirectly) have freely given feafon-
able Relief; for which, may God grant them

Bleffings in this World, and in the World to come everlafting Life, for Chrift's fake!

Now, God, in His great Mercy, hath granted me a temporal Salvation, and what is a Thoufand Times better, he hath given me with it, a Soul-fatisfying Evidence of an eternal in the World to come!

And now, what fhall I render to the Lord for all his Benefits, alas I am nonpluft! O that Saints and Angels might praife thee, for I am not worthy to take thy Name into my Mouth any more! Yet notwithftanding, thou art pleafed to accept poor Endeavours, becaufe *Jefus Chrift* has opened the Door, whereby we may come boldly to the Throne of thy Grace, praifed be the Lord God Jehovah, by Men and Angels, throughout all Eternity!

But to haften to the Conclufion, fuffer me with Humility and Sorrow to obferve, that our Enemies feem to make a better Ufe of a bad Religion, than we of a good One; they rife up long before Day in Winter, and go through the Snow in the coldeft Seafons, to perform their Devotions in the Churches; which when over, they return to be ready for their Work as foon as Day-Light appears: The Indians are as zealous in Religion, as the French, they oblige their Children to pray Morning and Evening, particularly at Conafadauga; are punctual in performing their ftated Acts of Devotion themfelves, are ftill and peaceable in their own Families, and among each other as Neighbours!

When I compared our Manner of Living with theirs, it made me fear that the righteous and jealous God (who is wont to make Judgment begin at his own Houfe firft) was about to deliver us into their Hands, to be feverely punifhed for our Departure from him; how long has he waited for our Return, O that we may therefore turn to him, before his Anger break out into a Flame, and there be no Remedy!

Our Cafe appears to me indeed very gloomy! notwithftanding our Enemies are inconfiderable in Number, compared with us; yet they are *united as one Man*, while we may be juftly compared to a Houfe divided againft itfelf, and therefore cannot ftand long, in our prefent Situation.

May Almighty God, gracioufly incline us to look to him for DELIVERANCE, to *repent* of our Sins, *reform* our Lives, and *unite* in the *vigorous* and *manly* Ufe of all proper Means to this End. Amen.

FINIS.

INDEX

A

NARRATIVE

OF THE

WONDERFUL ESCAPE

AND

DREADFUL SUFFERINGS

OF

COLONEL JAMES PAUL,

AFTER THE DEFEAT OF COL. CRAWFORD, WHEN THAT UNFORTUNATE
COMMANDER, AND MANY OF HIS MEN, WERE INHUMANLY BURNT
AT THE STAKE, AND OTHERS WERE SLAUGHTERED BY OTHER
MODES OF TORTURE KNOWN ONLY TO SAVAGES.

BY ROBERT A. SHERRARD.

PRINTED FOR J. DRAKE.

CINCINNATI:
SPILLER, PRINTER, VINE STREET.
1869.

INTRODUCTION.

THE object of the publisher of this narrative is two-fold: to preserve from oblivion the deeds of our ancestors, that the rising generation may be instructed and improved by their perseverance and triumphs over difficulties that surrounded them—and that the future historian may be furnished with material with which to do ample justice to our past history. The facts incidentally stated, that Colonel Paul was the uncle of the late Judge George Paul Torrence, the father of the present Mayor of the city of Cincinnati, and that he built on Brush Creek in Adams county, the pioneer furnace of Southern Ohio, and that Colonel James Paul was born in 1757; his father, George Paul, moved on the farm in 1768, and died in 1778; and that Colonel James Paul died July 9th, 1841, aged eighty-four years, and that he was twenty-five years old at the time of Crawford's defeat, and was unmarried, are facts that might be thought of but little importance to some, but the future historian may regard them as facts of inestimable value.

NARRATIVE

OF THE

WONDERFUL ESCAPE, ETC.,

OF COLONEL JAMES PAUL.

MY present intention in furnishing you for publication this copy of the narrative of Colonel James Paul's almost miraculous escape from the Sandusky Indians at the time of Colonel Crawford's defeat, is two-fold—to give the public and the many friends of Colonel Paul a true statement of that hair-breath escape, and in the second place to correct an error into which some writers have fallen, as to the motive of Colonel Crawford and his noble band of volunteers in going to Upper Sandusky, which object was in reality to whip the Wyandottes and bands of hostile Indians, and to burn their town; and not, as erroneously reported, to complete the slaughter of the remainder of the peaceable Christian Moravian Indians.

In the spring of 1782 a scheme was formed and put on foot, the object of which was to check the Sandusky Indians, principally that of the Wyandotte tribe, which tribe was at that time the most bold, daring, and ferocious of any of the other hostile tribes, whose depredations on the frontier settlers had grown hard to be borne.

A further object of the scheme was the destruction of the Indian town at Upper Sandusky, and thus to check and put a stop, if possible, to the scalping, murdering, and plundering which was continually committed by the hostile Indians on the defenseless settlers on the frontier of West Virginia and West Pennsylvania.

It is not true that the object of Colonel Crawford and his volunteer companies was to go to Upper Sandusky and slaughter and kill off the balance or remainder of the peaceable Moravian Indians, as stated by Weems and one other author, who have misstated the object of these brave, noble-hearted volunteers, who, under Colonel Crawford, risked their lives in an enemy's country. Surely it could not be the object of these men to go so far into an enemy's country for the sole purpose of completing the slaughter of a few remaining Moravian Indians, while they could turn their hands against the Wyandotte tribe and their hostile allies, and thereby perform a better service and do a nobler action. I will here let Colonel James Paul give his narrative of his hair-breadth escape from the Indians at the time of Crawford's defeat:

In the month of January, 1826, I called upon Colonel James Paul, and received a satisfactory statement of his narrow escape from the camp-ground of Upper Sandusky on his retreat homeward. In his report to me of Crawford's Campaign he contradicted the statement of Weems, particularly in that that it was not the scheme, or any part of it, for Colonel Crawford and his volunteers to go out and kill off the few remaining Christian Moravian Indians. Colonel Paul further stated to me that Weems made another misstatement where, in speaking of Colonel Crawford's volunteers, he says they were all volunteers from the immediate neighborhood of Ohio, except one company from Ten Mile, in Washington county, Pennsylvania; when the fact was, said Colonel Paul, they were all volunteers from Fayette county, Pennsylvania, from the east side of the Monongahela River, east of Brownsville, except one company from Ten Mile, in Washington county, Pennsylvania, and the command of the volunteers was given to Colonel Crawford, who marched the men from Benson, now Uniontown, on the 20th of May, 1782, on to Brownsville, then called Redstone Old Fort, where more volunteers joined us, and on the 22d of May we arrived at Cat Fish, now Washington, Pennsylvania, where more volunteers, a company from Ten Mile, joined us.

On the 24th we left Washington, Pennsylvania, and on the 25th arrived at the Ohio River, but did not cross until the 26th of May, 1782. Our volunteers then and there numbered four hundred and eighty-two men. We crossed the Ohio River at the old Indian Mingo town, and from there we took up over the hill and traveled on an old Indian trail near where the villages of Jefferson and Salem (now Anapolis) now stand, on the dividing ridge. We traveled on the ridge until

the Indian trail we traveled on intersected another trail
leading out from the Ohio River opposite where Wells-
burg now stands.   The Indian trail led us on westward
to the Moravian towns on the west side of the Muskingum river.   The names of these Moravian towns in
these days were Shonnenberg, Sharon, Goshen, and
Naden Hutten.   At all these Moravian towns silence
and desolation reigned ; all was desolation. owing to
the massacre of these peaceable Christian Indians by
Colonel Williamson's desperate set of insubordinate,
unpolished, half-civilized frontier settlers, in the month
of March, 1782, previous to our design of marching
out to destroy Wyandotte towns at Upper Sandusky.

These men, after they had murdered all the Christian
Moravian Indians, great and small, male and female,
that they could lay their hands on (and it is said none
escaped except an Indian boy ten or twelve years old,
by creeping out through a window while those fiends
were engaged in dispatching his relatives, and escaping
to the Wyandotte tribe at Upper Sandusky, conveying
the intelligence of the massacre to the hostile Indians),
set fire to the corn-cribs and burnt them up, together
with all their contents.   For it was considered necessary that the corn should be burnt or destroyed to prevent its falling into the hands of the Wyandottes, or
other hostile bands of marauding Indians.

After the news of the massacre of these peaceable
Christian Indians had spread abroad, it was strongly
denounced by the public generally, as an uncalled for
atrocity, and Colonel Williamson was severely censured
for suffering such a heinous offense to be committed

before his eyes, and that too by men under his command. It is true, these men were under the command of Colonel Williamson, but not under his control. They were a set of desperate, wicked, unprincipled men—frontier settlers; such men as may always be found upon the outskirts of civilization—men that bore a deadly hatred to all Indians of every tribe, and would neither be advised nor controlled by their commander but took the work into their own hands, and as any insubordinate set of men would do under such circumstances, regardless of consequences.

These men afterward strove to make the public believe, as a palliation of their wicked deed, that they had found clothing among these pet Indians that had been stripped off of their wives and daughters after they had been tomahawked and scalped by the Indians, and that the sight of these well-known articles of family clothing so exasperated and stirred up such a spirit of revenge in the bosoms of those men that Colonel Williamson had no control over them; they took the matter into their own hands, and these facts concerning the want of subordination were reported by the men who were present but took no part in the murder, but exonerated Colonel Williamson from all blame.

Our volunteers sauntered about the desolated Moravian town to see what they could see, and that was but little, except the extreme lonely aspect of the place, but in doing so one of the men picked up a good garden spade and concluded to carry it with him, saying it would be of service to bake bread on.

We left the Moravian towns on the 30th of May,

2

and nothing worthy of note occurred until after we
arrived on the Sandusky plains, which was on the 4th
day of June, where we camped, and on the 5th of June
the battle commenced, and was renewed on the 6th of
June, 1782.

On these two days the volunteers suffered very much
from extreme heat and the want of water, but our
company did not suffer for want of water as much as
others, for your father, with two canteens, carried
water to our company from where a large tree had
fallen out of root, and the opening made by the roots
filled with rain water, and from this reservoir he supplied our company at the risk of his life, as bullets
from the Indian rifles were flying all around us, and
sometimes wounding a comrade at the sapling or tree
where he stood.

Daniel Canon and two other men of our company,
filled with curiosity and the novelty of the situation,
climbed up into scrubby bushy-topped trees and shot
and killed, or wounded, several Indians secreted among
the long grass, for whenever an Indian raised his head
a little to see if he could get a shot at one of our men,
some one of these sharpshooters would pop away at
him from his hiding place in the tree-top.

Colonel Crawford and his men, after battling with
the Indians for near two days, and gaining nothing,
but losing a great many valuable lives. and fearing
that if they occupied their ground until next day it
might prove disastrous, as our ammunition and provisions were nearly exhausted.

Seeing that delay would be dangerous if not disas-

trous, a retreat was therefore ordered to take place by six
o'clock on the night of the 6th of June, to be conducted
with as much secresy as possible, leaving all the fires
burning so as to deceive the Indians, and in making preparations for the retreat, bread had to be baked, and for
that purpose some of the men had made use of a spade
picked up near the Moravian town on our way out.
The spade, while hot, had been thrown to one side, and
I happened to set my foot on it, and the bottom being
out of my moccasin, my foot was burned severely before I felt the pain.   For a while the pain was very
severe, but at length it became easy and I fell asleep;
but I suppose I could not have slept long, for the last
time I saw your father—till I saw him afterward at
home with my mother and sisters—he came to me and
gave me a shake, at the same time saying, "Jamy,
Jamy, up, and let us be off; the men are all going."
I sprang to my feet and stepped to the sapling where
my horse was tied, but to my sad disappointment my
horse had slipped his bridle.

I groped about in the dark and discovered two other
horses tied to the same sapling, and my horse standing
at their tails. This revived my drooping spirits. On finding my horse standing quiet, I bridled him and mounted,
and about the same time a number of other horses
were mounted by their owners, and all put out from
the camp ground together, amounting in all to nine in
number, and we made as much haste to get away as
we could, considering the darkness of the road, and no
roads but open woods to ride through, and no one to
guide us.   At this time the main body of the volun-

teers, under Colonel Williamson, were retreating on
what we considered not as nigh a course home, leaving
us nine and many other stragglers behind to take care
of themselves as best they could, and to steer their own
course homeward, and, as it turned out afterward, but
few of these stragglers ever got home. They were
either shot down and scalped, or, if made prisoners,
they were tortured in a cruel manner, and sometimes
burned at the stake. Hence, men who knew the
Indian custom of treating prisoners of war, would
rather suffer themselves to be shot or die by the blow
of a tomahawk, than to suffer more deaths than one by
torture. This was my determination when I sprang off
from my four remaining comrades and was chased by
two Indians for life, as I will shortly relate.

I and my eight comrades had not advanced far, perhaps not over a mile, on our retreat, until we all rode
into a large deep swamp. In this dismal swamp we
all got our horses deeply plunged into the mire, so
much so that we were compelled to dismount and take
to our feet, leaving our horses to be got out by the
Indians the next day or perish in the mire. As soon
as we dismounted from our horses in the swamp, we
were obliged to make our way as best we could by
stepping from one tussic or bunch of grass to another
all the way across the swamp. We had one little
fearful man with us, that ought to have stayed at home ;
he was too short in the legs to step at all times so as
to reach the next tussic—hence he would slip into the
mire and slush up to his armpits, and in this situation
he would work and toil to get out, but could not for a

while. He would then raise the hue and cry for help, and beg of us for God's sake not to leave him. His hallooing and bawling was so loud that I was afraid he would bring the Indians upon us; but by some means he got out of the swamp, and soon overtook us, well plastered with mud up to his armpits.

I made but a poor out at walking, owing to the bad burn on the sole of my foot, and the bottom being out of my moccasin. However, my spirit and anxiety to get home bore me up, and I walked on in much pain. We traveled all that night, and the next day till noon, without rest or food. After we had stopped to rest I took from my knapsack the piece of Indian blanket I had found on the camp ground the evening before, and tore off another strap and wrapped it round my foot over the burn, which, by this time became sore and much inflamed. But the piece of blanket proved of great service, for, as it would wear through on the sore, I would shift it round, and when one piece was worn out I would replace it with another, and in this manner preserved my foot, as much as possible, from injury. At this place we concluded to take some refreshment, as we had eaten nothing since the evening before.

The place where we stopped to dine was all over-grown with high weeds, which we broke down and spread a blanket on, then each man took from his little store of provisions a portion of his ash cake, baked on the camp ground the evening before, and laid it on the blanket, which served us instead of a table cloth. We commenced eating, and had ate but a short time, when the little fearful man, who had made such a noise in the swamp the night before, would be up by turns looking for Indians. At length he squatted down quickly, and in a low tone bade us hide. "There is Indians coming," he said. On hearing this, each man took his course and hid. For. my part, I took the direction toward the Indian trail, and concealed myself in a large bunch of alder bushes, where I had a full view of the Indians as they passed. All at once the foremost one on the trail stopped short, and that brought all the Indians behind him to a halt.

They were all mounted on Indian ponies, twenty-five in number, and it appeared as if the Indians had heard a rustling noise made by the men in their haste to hide, for as soon as the Indians brought their horses to a halt, they looked and gazed round about and appeared to be listening, fully intent upon catching any sound or noise that was made. But our men were all soon hidden among the high weeds, and a deathlike stillness followed. In a very short time, hearing no noise, the foremost Indian gave his horse two or three kicks on the side, and a whistle, and the rest following his example, moved off on a trot toward Sandusky, still keeping their order in Indian file. From the place of my concealment I had a full view of the twenty-five Indians who had given us such a scare, and caused us to hide. I could, with my rifle, have brought down any one of them, but I .durst not, knowing that it would have brought about my own destruction and that of my comrades, for every one of those Indians was armed with a rifle, and on their way to Upper Sandusky. I and my comrades were glad to be thus rid of their company.

As soon as those Indians had gone out of sight, I and my comrades returned to the spot where the blanket lay, and each man gathered up what belonged to him and stored it away for future use, not having any desire, at the time, to finish our dinner. The scare we had gotten from the presence of so many Indians, had the effect to make us feel satisfied that we had had, for the present, dinner enough, and we all started off on our course home, but could not shake off the fear of meeting Indians.

On the evening of the same day, being the 7th of June, 1782, while we were pursuing our way across a large space of open ground, we saw, at a considerable distance from us, running off to our right, a solitary Indian, but at too great a distance to shoot him. From this single Indian we apprehended no danger, but we afterward paid dearly for our security, as you shall hear. I remember that after my return home, on relating the circumstance of seeing this solitary Indian, it was suggested to me that we should have turned off at a right angle and steered northward for a few miles, and then have turned east again, and by that means evaded the Indians that might follow us. But my reply was, that men who were acquainted with the sagacity of the Indians know that it is hard to evade their pursuit. They track white men, and Indians too, on leaves, grass, or bare ground, and it is said they can distinguish between the white man's track and that of the Indian, when the white man could see no track at all.

But for the timebeing, we marched heedlessly on in

security, keeping on our course until dark. We then lay down to rest and slept soundly and securely, having had no sleep since the night of the 5th, and but little then.

On the morning of the 8th of June we pushed on in high spirits, believing, as we thought, we were leaving the camp ground and the Indians some miles behind.

This day, June 8th, 1782, about ten o'clock in the morning, we passed over a small hill and descended into a valley below, when we were fired upon by a party of Indians concealed in ambush on our right. I was walking so close to the man on my left that I could have laid my hand on his shoulder, he on the left, and I on the right, next to the Indians, and yet my comrade was shot dead the first fire. The ball must have passed very close to me, and I supposed the Indian aimed to kill both of us with the same shot. But he was taken and I was left. Four of our men out of the nine fell at the first fire, and four of the remaining five took shelter behind trees.

The Indians, after their first fire, rose to their feet and called out in broken English to surrender, and not a man of them should be hurt. But I could place no confidence in an Indian, so I therefore broke and ran off at the top of my speed; but after running about twenty rods, I thought of my comrades, and on looking round in that direction, beheld the remaining four men all dead. Two were struck down by the tomahawk, and the two that still remained fought bravely until overpowered by superior numbers. The Indians had it in their power at one time to have shot me before I had got out of gun-shot, and as I ran in a lame hobbling manner, they may have supposed that I could be easily taken a prisoner by running me down, and then have their sport burning me at the stake. But, thank God, in this they missed their aim. And just as I supposed their aim was to take me alive, so it turned out to be ; for just as soon as they had slaughtered my comrades, I saw two of perhaps their swiftest runners start after me at full speed. On seeing this I mended my gait. I now saw and considered my life was at stake for the first time during this campaign, and this thought infused more life, vigor, and energy into my frame, and made me soon forget my burnt foot, and cause me to gain ground as I advanced from my pursuers.

When they discovered I was gaining on them they shot at, but missed me. These shots only made me run the faster, hoping and expecting soon to be out of reach of bullets. It was not long after they fired at me until one of them turned back, and soon after the second and last one left the pursuit and turned back to his comrades, leaving the race all to myself, for which I was thankful, and soon slackened my speed, and continued to take it more moderate all my journey through, until I crossed the Ohio River and reached home.

The evening of the 8th of June, 1782, a day I came near losing my life, and on which I lost by the Indian tomahawk and rifle, eight of my companions, as night began to close in, I thought it prudent to look out a place of concealment, not knowing but some of the

3

Indians might be on my track all day. At length I found an old hollow log with a large cavity, into which I crept feet foremost, taking my gun in with me. Here in this retreat I rested and slept soundly till morning. This ended my third night out since I left the battle ground. On the morning of the 9th of June I left my place of concealment, much refreshed by sleep and rest, both of which I much needed, and again took my course for home. But at first I could hardly walk a step, my foot being so sore and much swollen and inflamed, from the manner in which the Indians forced me to use it the day before.

And now my provision was gone, and the only sustenance I had until I crossed the Ohio River was one young blackbird I had caught, and service berries at this time ripe and in many places plenty, on my way homeward. I now traveled at an easy rate, but my progress was much retarded owing to my lameness, and having to stop frequently to gather service berries for food; but I progressed slowly on, not forgetting to keep a sharp lookout for Indians, but saw no more of them till long after my return home.

In pursuing my homeward course I suppose I passed near where Mount Vernon, Knox county, now stands, where I struck the waters of Owl Creek, and passed down the same until near its junction with the Mohigan Creek.

High up on Owl Creek I struck an Indian trail, and soon discovered fresh signs of Indians having passed on toward Sandusky. This discovery caused me to alter my course, for I had no wish to keep the trail,

fearing I should meet Indians. Striking off from the
trail, I took the nighest route to Tuscarawas River.

After I left the trail at what I considered a safe distance, I sat down to rest, and not far off I saw a shelving rock, with abundance of dry leaves under it, which
I thought would be good place to rest for the night,
but was afraid it was too near the Indian trail, and
I concluded to travel that night and the next day,
that I might be as far out of reach of the Indians as
possible.

I rose to my feet and made the attempt to proceed
on my way, but after I had walked a few steps I
found that I could not travel now after dark, for my
head became dizzy, and I reeled and staggered like a
drunken man, and I found I could gain no headway,
so I gave up traveling that night and made my way
to the shelving rock. I was aware that my weakness
arose from a want of nourishing food. After I came
to the shelving rock, I was afraid to lay down without
first stirring up the leaves with my ramrod to find out
if snakes stayed among them, but hearing no noise
except what I made, I tumbled in, and slept well till
morning.

From this place I steered direct for the Tuscarawas
River, which, on my arrival, I found too deep to cross.
I turned up the stream till I came to a ripple, where
I stripped off all my clothes and tied them in a small
bundle, which I held in my left hand on the top of my
head, while I held my gun in my right hand above
the water. I then waded across the river, the water
in the deepest place being up to my neck. I soon

dressed and ascended the hill from the river.   At the
top of the hill I discovered an old Indian trading camp.
where, scattered over the ground, lay a great many
whisky kegs, and the staves of many more gone to
pieces.   How or whence so many kegs and a few old
whisky barrels had come or had been collected, I could
not conjecture, for I felt sure that the Indians had no
means of conveying them to that place at that time.
White men must have done it; but it appeared evident that the place had been used long since as a rendezvous for Indian drink and frolic.

Here, on this old camp ground, among the kegs and
staves, I concluded to stay all night, it being almost
sundown.   Finding the gnats and musquitoes were
likely to be troublesome, I struck up a fire—the first I
had enjoyed the benefit of since I left the camp-fires
on the plains.   The old dry staves served for fuel to
keep the fire up.   I ran some risks in kindling a fire
on a high hill in the Indian country, and on the very
ground where they had had many drunken frolics, but
I risked it, and no Indian was attracted to the fire to
harm me.

This night among the kegs was my fifth night out
from camp.   Early the next morning (the 11th of
June, 1782), after sleeping most of the night, I left
the old drinking ground and steered for the Ohio
River, and on the morning of the 12th of June I
arrived at said river a short distance above the mouth
of Wheeling Creek, not far above where the town of
Wheeling now stands.

Finding no chance of crossing at that place, I kept

up the river until I got a short distance above the
mouth of Rush Run, opposite Pumphrey's bar and
bottom. At this place I concluded to cross, and proceeded to construct a raft by tying old rails together
with bark peeled from white-walnut bushes. These
rails had floated down from the upper country, and
lodged against a large sugar-tree which had fallen from
the bank into the river. After I had completed my
raft I shoved it into the river, and having procured a
piece of shivered rail for a paddle, I took my gun in
my hand and crawled on my raft on my hands and
knees. I then paddled over to the Virginia shore safe.
I was never more thankful in my life, resting sure that
I was safe from the Indians.

Seeing a number of horses feeding on Pumphrey's
bottom, next the river, I was fully bent on riding one
of them. I took from my raft some of the bark and
formed a halter, and approached the horses and tried
to catch three or four of them, but not one would let
me lay my hand on it. At length I put the halter on
a poor old raw-boned mare, and gun in hand, I mounted
and took up the hill on a path that led me to an im-
provement with a cabin-house, and here, for the first
time since I left the Ohio River on my outward trip, I
heard the chickens crowing, but there were no inhabitants, and not even a dog to bark. But still keeping
on the path, I passed several improvements, at each of
which the fowls would crow, but still no dog to bark,
nor a human being to be seen.

At length the path led me to a fort in Virginia Short
Creek, and at the fort I found the neighbors had col-

lected for safety   Runners had been sent around to warn them that Colonel Crawford and his volunteers had been defeated, and it was expected that the Indians would be in, and would soon be at their old work of murdering, scalping, and plundering the defenseless inhabitants ; and here at this fort I found several of my comrades who had escaped from the battle ground at Sandusky Plains, and wandered in like myself, in safety, but had reached the fort before me.

I stayed at the fort till the next day, and there I procured a horse that I rode on to near Washington, Pennsylvania, where I had relatives living, and with them I stayed two nights, and from these relatives I got a passage on horseback to my own home, where, for several days nothing but gloomy expectation had been indulged in by my mother and sisters—they not knowing but I was killed and scalped by the Indians. Your father had arrived four days before me, and could give no satisfactory account of me, as he had not seen me after he awoke me at the camp-fire at retreating time on the night of the 7th of June, and I did not arrive home till the 15th of June, 1782.

And here ends the narrative of Colonel James Paul, whose narrative had never been penned down until I did it in the month of January, 1826.

POPULAR CULTURE IN AMERICA

1800-1925

An Arno Press Collection

Alger, Jr., Horatio. **Making His Way; Or Frank Courtney's Struggle Upward.** n. d.

Bellew, Frank. **The Art of Amusing:** Being a Collection of Graceful Arts, Merry Games, Odd Tricks, Curious Puzzles, and New Charades. 1866

Browne, W[illiam] Hardcastle. **Witty Sayings By Witty People.** 1878

Buel, J[ames] W[illiam]. **The Magic City:** A Massive Portfolio of Original Photographic Views of the Great World's Fair and Its Treasures of Art . . . 1894

Buntline, Ned [E. Z. C. Judson]. **Buffalo Bill; And His Adventures in the West.** 1886

Camp, Walter. **American Football.** 1891

Captivity Tales. 1974

Carter, Nicholas [John R. Coryell]. **The Stolen Pay Train.** n. d.

Cheever, George B. **The American Common-Place Book of Poetry,** With Occasional Notes. 1831

Sketches and Eccentricities of Colonel David Crockett, of West Tennessee. 1833

Evans, [Wilson], Augusta J[ane]. **St. Elmo:** A Novel. 1867

Finley, Martha. **Elsie Dinsmore.** 1896

Fitzhugh, Percy Keese. **Roy Blakeley On the Mohawk Trail.** 1925

Forester, Frank [Henry William Herbert]. **The Complete Manual For Young Sportsmen.** 1866

Frost, John. **The American Speaker:** Containing Numerous Rules, Observations, and Exercises, on Pronunciation, Pauses, Inflections, Accent and Emphasis . . . 1845

Gauvreau, Emile. **My Last Million Readers.** 1941

Haldeman-Julius, E[manuel].**The First Hundred Million.** 1928

Johnson, Helen Kendrick. **Our Familiar Songs and Those Who Made Them.** 1909

Little Blue Books. 1974

McAlpine, Frank. **Popular Poetic Pearls,** and Biographies of Poets. 1885

McGraw, John J. **My Thirty Years in Baseball.** 1923

Old Sleuth [Harlan Halsey]. **Flyaway Ned;** Or, The Old Detective's Pupil. A Narrative of Singular Detective Adventures. 1895

Pinkerton, William A[llan]. **Train Robberies, Train Robbers, and the "Holdup" Men.** 1907

Ridpath, John Clark. **History of the United States,** Prepared Especially for Schools. Grammar School Edition, 1876

The Tribune Almanac and Political Register for 1876. 1876

Webster, Noah. **An American Selection of Lessons in Reading and Speaking.** Fifth Edition, 1789

Whiteman, Paul and Mary Margaret McBride. **Jazz.** 1926